Ukraine Meets the American Empire

Ukraine Meets the American Empire

Terrance R. Hyten

Clovercroft Publishing

Dedication

To my wife, children and grandchildren who I love with all of my heart. Their future to live as I have is in jeopardy.

To past generations, especially the founding generation, on whose shoulders we still stand on as the world's greatest Democracy.

To future generations, whose future to live as I have in freedom is in serious doubt.

Contents

PROLOGUE

The 2022 Russian-Ukrainian military war is part of a larger ongoing international conflict. This conflict has been playing out between western—especially U.S. hegemonic interests—pitted against those of the former Soviet Union, now Russia, since World War II. More recently, the geo-political interests of Communist China in the world have entered the fray sandwiched between these two world's major nuclear powers. For American, Russian, and Chinese interests worldwide, Ukraine now represents the epicenter of this epic struggle. The United States, Russia, and China are the world's leading elite nuclear military powers. Together, they possess ninety percent of the world's nuclear arsenals. They represent the world's current hegemonic titans.

For both the winning and losing side, going forward, this conflict will become a major pivoting point changing the world's geopolitical structure with unpredictable consequences. In the advanced hi-tech world we live in, multiple nations now possess hypersonic missiles, advanced drone technology, artificial intelligence, and coming digital currency. The face of almost everything is rapidly changing. For all sides, the stakes are extremely high.

Although this conflict appears limited to the battlefield in Ukraine it is not. It possesses all the characteristics of a major world war. This conflagration has already enveloped many of the world's major military powers; Iran, North Korea, and all thirty-one NATO nations, including Turkey, is heavily involved in the war. Finland's decision to join NATO was directly triggered by Russia's incursion, which expanded NATO's military commitments and guarantees.[1] Sweden is also petitioning to join the NATO alliance for the same reason. The entire world is feeling the effects of western sanctions against Russia. These armed hostilities have joined together Russian and Chinese interests to oppose America's international interests like no other event before could hope to have accomplished. The world's geo-political fault-line now lies thru American/NATO interests on one side and Chinese/Russian interests on the other.

The world's existing monetary order is also in upheaval with wars handmaiden—inflation running rampant around the globe. The continued role that the U.S. Dollar plays as the reserve currency in the world has also been placed at risk.[2] The Ukrainian conflict is accelerating the U.S. dollars demise as the world's dominant reserve currency. This is perhaps the most consequential result of the conflict, an event completely unforeseen by America's foreign policy establishment before entering the conflict in earnest in 2022.

The real causes triggering this Russian-Ukrainian military conflict are easily identifiable when one takes time to sit down and examine the cold facts. Understanding these root causes reveals which side is primarily at fault and the major foreign policy blunders that were made by both sides leading up to the war. After this analysis is undertaken, one can confidently predict the outcome of the current conflict. Further, one can begin to anticipate how the structure of the world's geopolitical alignment of nations will change going forward. Let's dive in.

SECTION ONE:

THE HISTORICAL BACKGROUND TO THE CONFLICT

America's decision to voluntarily enter the Russian-Ukrainian military conflict on the Ukrainian side represents yet another chapter of military intervention of its own choosing in a far distant country. Despite obvious close historical ties between Russia and Ukraine going back centuries, ethnic and cultural factors, and the geographical reality that Ukraine is located directly in Russia's backyard, America chose to become deeply involved in Ukraine's internal and international affairs. This decision was made despite repeated warnings by Russia for more than a decade that to do so would risk precipitating a major war with them.

America's decision to intervene in Ukraine's military conflict with Russia was made nearly a decade ago in 2014.[3] At this time, Ukraine had already disintegrated into Civil War and Russia had sent its military across borders to seize Crimea. Since 2014 the West has been supplying Western Ukraine with vast amounts of military aid.[4] These previous events are the progenitor which caused the Russians to intervene in Ukraine in 2022. American foreign policy think-tank experts saw as an opportunity to leverage the civil war in Ukraine to America's advantage. Russian influence in the region could be weakened further and NATO could expand closer to Russian borders also accruing to the West advantage. However, these events which are contributing to the current military conflagration are now conveniently ignored by the West. Certainly, both American and NATO promises made to Ukraine to provide massive amount of military assistance discouraged negotiations that would have led to an early end to the conflict in 2022 shortly after the Russian military crossed its borders.

Attempts to negotiate a settlement were made between these two warring sides, however these efforts were squelched by Western interference in both Washington D.C. and London. Purportedly, a negotiated interim settlement was reached between Russia and Ukraine in early April 2022, but the settlement process was stopped dead in its tracks in the West. Decision makers in both the United States and Britain strongly urged Ukraine not to compromise and reach a settlement with Russia.[5] Instead, increased military support was promised to Ukraine by NATO.

For hegemonic reasons, the West wanted the proxy war against Russia to continue. Russia had to be taught a major lesson concerning its unacceptable behavior in the international community. Russia needed to be reeled in by the scuff of its neck and compelled to comply with established rules of international order. The war in Ukraine would accomplish these ends. At least this is the official American position.

So, what are America's real strategic interests in Ukraine and what is Russia's? Geography provides a good partial answer to this very important question. Based upon geography alone it is logical that Russia's strategic interests in Ukraine are vital and arguably existential. This is especially so if Ukraine was ever granted membership into NATO. If NATO forces and weapons are placed only ten miles or so from the Russian border, it is understandable why Russia is nervous and resists this outcome. And let's face it—NATO is almost entirely a U.S. controlled organization.[6]

Geography and distance matter in warfare. The distance between the U.S. and Kiev is 4,900 miles. The distance between Kiev and the Russian border is less than 300 miles. Two vast oceans separate the US and Ukraine whereas Russia and Ukraine share a common border of nearly 1,500 miles. But NATO, led by America, has decided to challenge Russia militarily on the ground in Ukraine and risk expanding the domestic Ukrainian civil conflict into a major world war in order to do so.

America's intentional disregard of this reality also ignores the complex nature of the region's history and displays extreme Yankee hubris whose underlying motivation is bent on preserving its own world hegemony. When the history of the region is considered along with America's ulterior motives for intervening, the error of American foreign policy becomes all too evident. And a closer look reveals that the major military conflict in Ukraine was completely avoidable, but for a multitude of Western policy mistakes that were made beginning shortly after the end of the first Cold War. These mistakes are continuing to compound today. This conflict will have major repercussions for the future of the world's order, and for America for a very long time.

CHAPTER ONE:

The Historical Backdrop Matters

There are historical ties between Russia and Ukraine going back more than eight hundred years. Due to their proximity, these countries share a similar culture and common history. Large areas and cities within Ukraine have deep Russian roots.[7] The Russian language is spoken in many of Ukraine's regions—especially in the Eastern region in Ukraine known as the Donbas region. Almost sixty percent of Crimea is ethnically Russian and speak Russian instead of Ukrainian.[8] Sevastopol, the largest Russian naval base on the Black Sea, is located in Crimea. It has been under Russian control serving as an important naval military base for Russia since 1776.[9] Both Odessa and Kiev are culturally ancient Russian cities dating back centuries.[10] In fact, Ukraine only recently gained its complete independence from the former Soviet Union in December 1991. For centuries, Ukraine has been subjugated by many of its neighbors. Again, and in stark contrast, most American's do not have the ability to find Ukraine on a world map—unless of course you're Hunter Biden.

Ukraine's recent history reveals a nation that is truly divided. Ukrainian nationalism is much stronger in Western Ukraine than in its Eastern region, and speaking generally, Western Ukrainians desire closer ties with Western Europe than with Russia.[11] During WWII, these regions split their support between opposing sides, aiding either Germany or Russia.[12] When Adolf Hitler invaded this area at the beginning of WWII, Nazi troops were enthusiastically welcomed in Kiev. Many Ukrainians waved banners raising their right arms with celebratory heil Hitler salutes applauding the goose-stepping Nazi troops who were invading their nation. Collaboration between the Nazi Regime in Germany with many Western Ukrainians is well documented.[13] Historically, as many as one and a half million Jews lost their lives in this area during the early stages of WWII in what is known as the holocaust of bullets.[14] Many Ukrainians, especially in the Western region, actively participated in these atrocities savagely perpetrated against the Jewish population. Bluntly stated, they sided with the NAZI regime to commit genocide against a defenseless Jewish population.

A rather sizable Nazi influence remains today in Western Ukraine camouflaged in the guise of Ukrainian nationalism. Today, the Ukrainian army boasts that its AZOV battalions, many sporting swastika tattoos and Nazi insignia, are among the best in their military.[15] National Monuments dedicated to Stepan Bandera are commonly seen throughout Ukraine prominently displayed in main thoroughfares in cities and towns.[16] Bandera was an ardent nationalist with documented Nazi beliefs, sympathies with ties to Germany's Nazi fascist regime.[17] He also strongly opposed Communism, Bolshevism, and despised Russian influence in Ukraine. Bandara hated everything Russian. Bandera's birthday is still celebrated every year as a Ukrainian national holiday.[18] Certainly, if the goal of America's foreign policy is to weaken Russia and potentially overthrow Putin's rule, then Ukraine is almost the most perfect ally to select to do so.

In contrast, Eastern Ukraine, especially the Donbas region and Crimea, have a closer ethnic affinity with Russia.[19] During the Bolshevik Revolution in 1917, unlike Western Ukraine, there was considerable support for its cause in the Eastern Ukrainian region. During WWII, most of the population in Eastern Ukraine favored the Russian side instead of Western Ukrainians who supported NAZI Germany.[20] After the collapse of the Soviet Union in 1991, Eastern provinces in Ukraine voted strongly in favor of candidates who preferred to maintain close ties with Russia whereas in Western Ukraine the opposite was true.[21]

In fact, most of the population living in Eastern Ukraine support closer ties with Russia rather than the West.[22] In the first decade after 2000, more than eight million ethnic Russians lived in Ukraine, especially clustered together in the Donbas region in Eastern Ukraine and in Crimea.[23] These deep ethnic divisions have largely caused the ongoing civil war between Western Ukraine against the breakaway regions in the Donbas in Eastern Ukraine to develop into the full-scale war we are witnessing today.

Ukraine's recent history encompassing WWII and its aftermath needed to be taken account when implementing American foreign policy in the region —but it wasn't. Or probably worse, American foreign policy experts were aware of these underlying deep ethnic divisions existing in Ukraine and decided to take advantage of them. American foreign policy has a penchant for interfering in the internal affairs of many other sovereign nations without adequately assessing historical ethnic and socio-economic contours of the region before doing so. A strong case can be made that America too often meddles in the internal affairs of other nations solely for its own benefit and is simply engaging in a modern version of medieval feudalism.

In summary, Ukraine's recent history reveals a nation that's divided ethnically and politically between East and West. Ukraine's internal conflict was easily exploitable by the West if they chose to do so. And as early as the mid to late 1990's the West decided to do so. Once the West intervened militarily throwing the full weight of its support to one side over the other, positions on each side solidified and battlelines were drawn. The very nature of NATO choosing sides creates another underlying reason that the current Russian Ukrainian civil war has expanded into wide open conflict between Russia and the West. Succinctly stated, NATO expansion towards Russian borders, especially in Ukraine, is a major culprit driving the military conflict between itself, Ukraine, and Russia.

CHAPTER TWO:

The Post-Soviet Era and NATO Expansion

Since the fall of the Berlin Wall in 1989, eight of the former Soviet occupied countries and two other nations have aligned with the West assimilating into the welcoming wide-open arms of NATO.[24] Additionally, East Germany, a former Soviet satellite, reunited with West Germany in 1990 to form the most potent economic powerhouse in Europe. Altogether, NATO expansion now encompasses thirty-one nations and has almost tripled in size since 1991 to Russia's obvious alarm. It also significantly increases the scope of NATO's geographic area to defend, and respective military commitments pledged in the event of war. Stated again with great emphasis, NATO's expansion east, towards Russian border, greatly concerns Russia.[25]

Most of NATO's new members at one time were Soviet satellite nations. There is little doubt but that NATO expansion toward Russia intends to preclude any Russian ambition to expand again beyond its historic borders. There is also little doubt but that another goal the West desires to achieve is to diminish Russian influence thru usurping Russian economic ties with its former satellites, gain market share in its favor in the region and weaken Russia's economy and military. Even earlier in 2008, NATO recruited Ukraine to become a member of the NATO alliance and fully integrated into the EU pulling Ukraine away from its historic ties with Russia.[26] The significance of NATO's recruitment of Ukraine to become a member cannot be overstated. This lies at the heart of the matter and is the primary cause of the current military conflict between Russia and Ukraine.

These geopolitical readjustments have occurred at a time when the Western elite who shape foreign policy in the post-Soviet era believe Russia is in a weakened condition unable to oppose Western military expansion into Eastern Europe. Stated more directly, when the Soviet Empire collapsed in 1991, Russia was in such an embarrassingly weakened condition that it had little, if any, capability to present a significant military challenge to NATO nations. In fact, after the collapse of the Soviet Empire in the early 1990's, the original NATO nations themselves were internally divided struggling to find its identity and purpose going forward. There was considerable debate at that time inside NATO whether it should continue to exist as a defensive alliance at all[27]. Obviously, the Soviet Union no longer posed a major military threat to Western Europe. The once formidable Soviet Empire had imploded into a weak vessel of its former self. It was truly a paper tiger that had been rotting from within for decades.

The primary purpose for NATO's existence as an alliance had collapsed just as rapidly as the collapse of the Berlin Wall. Putin even indicated a willingness to join the NATO alliance shortly after the breakup of the former Soviet Union.[28] In essence, a once formidable enemy that threatened European security ceased to be a major threat and NATO's original purpose vanished overnight after the fall of the Berlin Wall.

After a lengthy internal debate, NATO made the momentous decision to expand the size and scope of NATO and to alter its original mission.[29] NATO's modified mission statement now implicitly includes bringing former Soviet satellite nations into NATO's network, integrating them with Western economies, and forging military allegiances tied to the West instead of Russia. Due to NATO's aggressive expansion east, the seeds of future military conflict between Russia and the West were already being sown decades ago.

So why has NATO expanded eastward into Russia's backyard increasing the size and scope of its protective military umbrella when NATO's express purpose to exist as a defensive bulwark against the former Soviet Union aggression is admittedly greatly diminished? The Russians of course feel threatened and have strongly objected to NATO's continuing expansion towards it borders. Until recently, Russia has only conceded to this expansion due to the reality of its weakened condition and military impotence unable to counter NATO's advances eastward.

Additionally, Russia simply believed that the Cold War with the West was over when conceding defeat to the West in 1991. When the Berlin Wall was dismantled and the collapse of the Soviet Union became a reality, an era of European peace was within reach. A new era of cooperation between Russia and the West was achievable. At least the Russian's thought so.

But Russia was far too optimistic, and in retrospect naïve, to think that relations with the collective West would improve on anything other than strictly Western terms.

Further, Russian President Mikhail Gorbachev received assurances during the first Bush Administration that NATO would not expand into former Soviet satellite nations.[30] Purportedly, James Baker, the former U.S. Secretary of State to President George HW Bush, told former Soviet President Mikhail Gorbachev, the Soviet Union's last leader, in February 1990, that NATO would not expand "not one inch more" towards Russia shortly after the fall of the Berlin Wall.[31] However, subsequent American administrations conveniently ignore this mutual understanding. In retrospect, this critical understanding between Russia and the West should have been formalized. The Russian side made a crucial error by not insisting that a formal declaration be drawn and signed by all interested parties. This is a mistake the West continues to exploit to its advantage.

Unfortunately, American promises made to their counterparts in Russia concerning NATO expansion have been repeatedly broken. This in turn has led to Russia's mistrust towards the West making a negotiated settlement in this current military conflict even more difficult to achieve. Is it possible that NATO's continual mission creep eastward since 1991 toward the Russian homeland, led by American foreign policy more than doubling the size of NATO, is a major cause of the Ukrainian military conflict?[32]

This is an extremely important question. It demands an answer from America and the West. Putin asked this very question in 2007 during an important Munich Security Conference whose agenda included a discussion revolving around joint European cooperation and security. His words are prescient today:

> "It turns out that NATO has put its frontline forces on our borders... I think that it is obvious that NATO expansion does not have any relation with the modernization of the alliance itself or with ensuring the security of Europe. On the contrary, it represents a serious provocation that reduces the level of mutual trust."[33]

Putin distinctly identified Russian distress over NATO expansion decades ago.

The nations joining NATO after the collapse of the Soviet Union: Poland, Hungary, Romania, Czechoslovakia, Bulgaria, Estonia, Latvia, Lithuania, Slovakia, Slovenia, Albania, and Croatia, do not physically border Russia. However, Ukraine does.[34] For this reason, Russian President Vladimir Putin made it very clear as early as 2008 that Russia would not allow Ukraine to join the NATO alliance.[35] The West was repeatedly warned by Russia that this is a red line which, if crossed, would lead to direct confrontation between Russia and the West. Putin has consistently and unequivocally stated Russia's position that Ukraine was a red line not to be crossed by the West without triggering a probable major military conflict.[36]

For more than a decade, Putin along with other high ranking Russian diplomats did attempt to negotiate a peaceful resolution to this considerable impasse in Ukraine. However, these diplomatic efforts were rebuffed in the decision-making centers in Washington DC, Brussels', and London.[37] Half-hearted negotiations did bear some fruit when the Minsk Accords were entered into in 2014 to end the conflict between Russia and Ukraine in the Donbas region. However, German

Chancellor Angela Merkel recently admitted that the West did not enter into these agreements with Russia in good faith. Merkel added that NATO was merely "buying time" to enable the West to arm the Ukrainian military against Russia.[38] The veracity of her words have been echoed and confirmed by the former French President Francois Hollande admitting that he and Merkl had lied to their Russian counterparts when negotiating the Minsk Protocols.[39] In other words, the EU or Ukrainian governments never seriously intended to live by the actual terms of the Minsk Accords. The West only agreed to the framework of this settlement agreement and signed on the dotted line to gain an upper hand in the event of any future military conflict with Russia. Ironically, it is the West's duplicity in this regard that has led to open military conflict and probable defeat of Ukraine at the hands of the Russians.

Furthermore, Vladimir Putin has voiced very few objections to full trade arrangements made between Ukraine and the West. He only insisted that Ukraine remain a major trading partner with Russia on an equal footing and act as a buffer—neutral zone—between Russia and NATO members.[40] Throughout this entire time frame, Russia's primary demand has been consistent. That is, Russia insists that Ukraine would not be recruited by the West to join NATO, but continue to play its critical role and act as a buffer zone between Russia and NATO, similar to the way Austria, and until recently, Finland had been doing so for decades.[41] This workable framework had been successfully proven to be an effective policy to avoid open conflict between Russia and NATO for decades in both Finland and Austria. However, maintaining this status quo in Ukraine was not to America's liking.

Russia was also alarmed by Ukraine's policy to purge the lives of many ethnic Russians residing in the Eastern Donbas region. Too often, ethnic Russians living in Ukraine were being poorly treated as second-class citizens by the Ukrainians. Worse, too often they were brutally murdered by Western Ukrainian paramilitary units aligned with a revitalized NAZI ideology with Kiev's tacit approval.[42] These atrocities that were committed against ethnic Russians in Ukraine are well documented. The West adamantly denies Vladimir Putin's accusations that some within Ukrainian government harbor ideological beliefs which are aligned with Nazism. Yet there is at least a kernel of truth in Putin's assertion.

After the collapse of the Soviet Union in 1991, an honest assessment of Ukraine's history in Eastern Europe reveals that it is NATO that has been aggressively expanding east towards Russian borders. NATO has almost tripled in size SINCE the collapse of the former Soviet Union. Organized shortly after WWII with twelve founding members, NATO was created to act solely as a defensive alliance.[43] NATO's sole purpose identified in its charter was to counter any military threat coming from the former Soviet Union.[44] These original NATO nations banded together and pledged a military alliance to counter offensive incursions instigated against any member by enemy military forces. Article Five in the NATO treaty dictates that an attack against any NATO nation would constitute an attack against every NATO nation.[45] Thus, all NATO member nations are committed to come to the aid and defend against the offensive onslaught from any foreign power.[46]

However, Ukraine is not a member of NATO and has NO official defense alliance with the west. There is certainly no treaty or military alliance obligating America or any other Western power to intervene on Ukraine's behalf regarding its current military conflict with Russia. So at least from Russia's vantage point, America's decision to either directly or indirectly insert itself into the current military Ukrainian conflict is naturally clouded with considerable suspicion that it is doing so for other ulterior reasons. And Russia presumes that these Western motives are hostile.

CHAPTER THREE:

America's Involvement in Ukraine

American involvement in Ukraine began almost immediately after WWII. The CIA has been involved in Ukraine since 1946 to bolster Ukrainian resistance against Soviet expansion and prevent the spread of Communism shortly after that world war. The operation is known in espionage circles as Operation Red-Sox.[47] During the Cold War this clandestine activity, spearheaded by the CIA, included making illegal airdrops of Ukrainian infiltrators, saboteurs, and guerrillas into the Soviet Union. Operating from a secure base in New York City, the Ukrainian resistance movement continued its struggle against the formerly formidable Soviet Empire until its complete collapse in 1991.[48]

U.S. foreign policy considers Ukraine and other Southern European émigré resistance groups as valuable assets designed to oppose the Soviet Union and the spread of communism into Western Europe for more than half a century. This policy now attempts to block Russian influence in the region decades after the Cold War has been won. In other words, America's relationship with Ukraine has been a useful instrument to oppose Russian aggression into the heart of Europe remaining intact since the end of WWII.

When one closely examines the way American foreign policy elites play the game of realpolitik on the world stage and the craftiness American policy wonks deftly move individual pieces—nations—around, clearly American operatives have been operational in the entire Eastern region of Europe and Central Asia since the late 1940's. They have done so to bolster their own strategic interests. The end goal has always been the same: to checkmate any ambitions of the former Soviet Union—now Russian—influence and to penetrate and control the Eastern regions of Europe. America and its allies also desire to reap enormous economic benefits from harvesting the abundant natural resources in this area. Russia alone is almost twice the size of America with vast untapped mineral resources. And American hegemonic elite do not tolerate direct competition against their interests very well anywhere in the world.

After the fall of the Soviet Union in 1991, American involvement in the region significantly increased. It targeted almost every former Soviet bloc nation for integration into the Western sphere of influence and attempted to pull them away from the Russia's sphere of influence. The list of these nations America has attempted to move around the chess board against Russian influence in this region is rather long—

Ukraine, Georgia, Armenia, Azerbaijan, Kazakhstan, Belarus, and even tiny Moldova.[49] Not only do these nations contain vast valuable mineral resources, they are geographically located on and near Russian borders which if brought into NATO's orbit would allow for the eventual complete military encirclement of Russia by the suffocating tentacles of NATO military forces. If Russia controls this large swathe of earth-almost twice the size of America-this would enable Russia to challenge American hegemony in both Europe and Asia.[50] As far as American strategic interests are concerned, this outcome must be avoided at all costs.

There is another crucial factor to consider. Unless Russia poses a real threat to America and its allies in Europe, American strategic interest in Ukraine is minimal at best. Shortly before the outbreak of the current military conflict in February 2021, American annual exports of goods and services to Ukraine was a measly $2.85 billion representing less than .00125 percent of total American exports that year. Annual imports from Ukraine as a percentage of total imports into the U.S. were even less significant to U.S. interests.[51] It would have been inconsequential for America if it had chosen not to intervene in the conflict on Ukraine's behalf.

Unfortunately, America has chosen instead to intervene in yet another nation halfway around the globe with whom it has no historical and cultural ties and with inconsequential trade. This alone, casts serious doubt concerning the veracity of America's officially stated position that it is intervening in Ukraine only to support the growth of Ukrainian Democracy and enforce the rules of international order against Russia's alleged unprovoked and illegal aggression. However, the veneer of America's self-appointed role to act as the world's sheriff with its self-determined purpose to spread its special brand sauce of democracy is beginning to wear thin among many government circles throughout the world.

America's direct involvement in the Ukrainian conflict significantly increases the duration of this war. Ergo, the American decision to entangle itself in Ukrainian military engagement increases casualties on both the Russian and Ukrainian side even though the ultimate outcome in Russia's favor is highly predictable. There is certainly a significant downside for both Ukraine and Russia due to America's involvement in their long-running regional squabbles. The lives of hundreds of thousands of soldiers are being extinguished on both sides which significantly impacts population growth for generations to come in both Ukraine and Russia.

Further, the very existence of Ukraine's ability to act as an independent sovereign nation is also being placed seriously at risk. It's apparent that America hasn't entirely abandoned its policy to oppose Russian geopolitical interests that existed during the Cold War. In fact, just the opposite has occurred. Since the mid 1990's, American policy has, inadvertently or intentionally, established a second cold war front against Russia in these former Soviet republics, a conflict now in danger of expanding into a hot and catastrophic worldwide war. The hounds of war are barking noticeably louder today in Europe than at any time since WWII. And most of these hounds seem to be barking more loudly by the unleashed dogs originating from the West than from Russia.

CHAPTER FOUR:

Russia's Involvement in Ukraine

Ukraine has been embroiled in considerable conflict and military conquest for centuries. During recent times going back a few centuries, it has been part of or controlled by Poland, Romania, and especially Russia. For a lengthy period, Russia and Ukraine were part of the same nation.[52] Ukraine only gained full independence from foreign powers since 1991 after the breakup of the former Soviet Union. Rightly or wrongly, Putin believes that Ukraine and Russia are united together as one people and it is undeniable that both are ethnically Slavic.[53] When Russia invaded Ukraine in early 2022, more than two million ethnic Russians living in Ukraine decided to flee north across the border into Russia instead of fleeing east to its Western NATO neighbors.[54]

Shortly after World War II the Soviet Union, whose forces had already swept thru and seized control of Ukrainian territory, set about to reinforce a strict regimen of ideological control over Ukraine. Significant attacks against Ukrainian historical culture took place. Many Ukrainians were deported to gulags in Siberia.[55] During this time, there was certainly a broad assault against Ukrainian culture. Numerous well documented atrocities occurred. Serious attempts by the Politburo were made to suppress Ukrainian heritage.[56] Now, Ukraine is attempting to return the favor against many of the ethnic Russians living in Ukraine. It has engaged in many of these same cruel acts perpetrated against them in the recent past to reassert control in the areas more aligned historically with Russian interests. America has intentionally inserted herself into the middle of this hornet's nest.

Yet throughout the Cold War, major forces were at work for a significant change of direction in virtually all the Soviet Union satellite nations. Their respective citizens yearned to be free and desired to gain independence, principally driven by poor performing state run economies and suppression of basic human liberties from the unfavorable effects of Communism. After the collapse of the Soviet Union, Ukrainians voted overwhelmingly in 1991 for their independence.[57] From that point forward, Ukraine's gradual movement towards integration with the West and NATO has begun in earnest in the post-Soviet era.

However, Ukraine's realignment with the West did not necessitate the complete coupling of both an economic and military union with both the EU and NATO. Yet, Western policy elites fully insisted that this coupling in fact occurred. Naturally, the West's coupling of both economic and military components regarding integration of the former Warsaw pact nations with the West threatens Russian interests. This further demonstrates the collective West geopolitical desires to favorably position itself to negate Russia's strategic interests in the area. America in particular gains an extreme economic advantage in its economic relationship with the EU when European trade with Russia is stifled in this manner. Large American international conglomerates can continue to profitably expand and increase their market share in Europe and Asia at Russia's expense. NATO also gains enhanced military capabilities to control the Black Sea and protrude into Russia's southern flank. It is pure and simply a play for control of vast undeveloped resources and reaping profits from them. As a bonus, NATO gains leverage in the Black Sea against Russian Naval forces in the event of war. It is also a move to checkmate Russia's navy in the region.

Eventual military conflict between NATO and Russia was inevitable unless a compromise could be reached, a compromise which would ensure military security to each side. The reasonable solution to this major obstacle to secure peace in Eastern Europe and Central Asia was obvious to anyone desiring regional stability. To establish a neutral zone between the former Cold War antagonists makes perfect sense and former Soviet satellite nations were well-suited to do so. These nations would function as buffer zones between the two former cold war antagonists. However, since this was the solution Russia embraced, the West curtly rejected it out of hand. There would be no compromise made with Russia. As far as American elites are concerned, any future conflict would be decided solely on American and NATO terms. Period, full stop. The West presumed that Russia too weak to resist NATO expansion.

The collective West further chose to ignore known psychological conditioning of the Russian psyche feeding Russian paranoia regarding its past historical experiences. These past national experiences seep deep into the average Russian citizens subconsciousness. Previous invasions by Western nations including the invasion by Emperor Napoleon from France in 1812, and more recently NAZI Germany and Hitler in 1941, magnified the perceived danger from the West's military mission creeping towards Russia's borders. Russian casualties resisting against NAZI Germany's invasion across its borders during World War Two exceeded twenty million citizens.[58] Yet, NATO continued in its quest to expand eastward toward Russia's borders feeding its national paranoia despite loud Russian protests attempting to stop NATO'S advance.

Once the West began in earnest to expand NATO towards Russian borders, an eventual showdown between the West and Russia was not only predictable but probable. Even though Russian protests grew progressively louder and louder, the collective West continued to disregard these warnings. Instead, the West continued to advance its aggressive expansionist policies. It pressed hard against Russia's borders playing havoc with the nationalist Russian psyche as well as its fragile paranoia state of mind. Inevitably, at some juncture Russian foreign policy would be forced to either readjust and accept this reality or decide to forcibly resist NATO's expansion. America and NATO expansion forced Russia's hand and provoked a response to the West's actions. The Russian response was entirely predictable.

CHAPTER FIVE:

America's Information Warfare Against Russia

There was a considerable amount of misreported news coverage during the Vietnam War. Today's storylines regarding the Ukrainian conflict should trigger luminous flashbacks in the memories of the baby boomer generation. These recollections would reflect carbon copy reruns of documented misreported media news coverage occurring during most of the Vietnam War era. Regrettably, most Americans have limited short-term memories concerning past historical events. It is certainly an American trait to forget or ignore large segments of its own history. Americans have largely forgotten the lessons learned in Vietnam. So, the saying goes, those who forget the lessons of history often end up repeating the same old mistakes.

The Pentagon Papers were published by the New York Times in 1971.[59] This explosive investigative reporting by the Times reporter Daniel Ellsberg stripped bare the hard unvarnished truth regarding the depth of the U.S. government and military lies repeatedly reported to the American people during the Vietnam War.[60] This exposé also showcases the ease the majority of American's were propagandized and misled by government leaders to garner continued support at home for that costly war.[61] They revealed that the U.S., without congressional knowledge or consent, and illegally, had secretly enlarged the Vietnam conflict thru running military operations into Cambodia and Laos.[62] The Pentagon Papers also revealed that the government's official version provided to the American public to support the war, to secure a non-Communist independent South Vietnam and to defend Democracy, was pure spin and BS. The Pentagon Papers reveals the hard truth that the American Government often lies to its citizens concerning its true foreign policy objectives overseas.

Contrary to the massive mainstream media narrative spun throughout most of the Vietnam era, the real reason the U.S. became militarily involved in Vietnam was simply to contain Communist China and Russia to prevent the further expansion of Communism.[63] The ring of this narrative should sound remarkably familiar to you today. This narrative is merely an echo chamber of false pronouncements made by past administrations. Americans are again being told that Russia is the aggressor invading Ukraine without any provocation. Americans are also being told that if Russia is allowed to achieve military victory in Ukraine, Russia's next objective will be to once again invade its NATO neighbors to reestablish the old Soviet Empire in Eastern Europe.[64] This is the same worn-out contrived narrative that was played repeatedly during the depth of the Vietnam War and the Cold War. Unfortunately, many Americans still swallow this line bait hook, line, and sinker.

The domino theory was believed to be a valid postulate justifying American involvement during the Vietnam era. Unfortunately, the reasoning of this questionable premise has conveniently resurfaced. It is now known in American government circles that the Soviet Union and Warsaw Pact nations never intended to invade Western Europe during the first Cold War.[65] Further, the Soviet Union ceased to exist in 1991 and Russia is no longer controlled by Communist ideology. The formidable Soviet Empire has collapsed, taking with it as well its core communist ideological commitment to undermine Capitalism throughout the world. Today, Russia is an awkward political hybrid mix between Democracy and Oligarchy. Russia now exemplifies most characteristics that a capitalist society does. That is not to say that Russian foreign policy interests are benign, only that they do not threaten American interests in North America.

But is there any validity to the Domino Theory? Certainly, one cannot have it both ways. Either Russia is too weak militarily to prevent NATO expansion towards its borders or strong enough to pose a definite threat to Ukraine as well as its closest NATO neighbors. If Russia is too weak militarily, then it poses no real threat to NATO. There is no need for NATO to expand eastward towards Russia. No dominos will fall in the West due to Russian aggression. American foreign policy, since the fall of the Berlin Wall, has been based upon the assumption of Russian weakness.

If, however, Russia does pose a real military threat to the West, why provoke Russia into direct military conflict thru engaging in aggressive expansionist policies in the first place.

A serious military challenge to NATO expansion by Russia should be expected. Why not instead attempt to reach a compromise with Russia to expand the economy of the EU without positioning NATO forces into former Soviet Satellite nations. The art of diplomacy is to avoid military conflict not to increase the odds that armed conflict will occur. The dominos are falling, but oddly they are falling instead in the direction of Russian borders due to NATO's continuing aggression. The Russian government clearly sees the reality of this situation.

The official U.S. government narrative regarding Ukraine is much of the same old worn-out false spin on reality. This subterfuge is easily refuted by anyone with a keyboard, access to the internet and a logical mind capable of connecting the dots and drawing reasonable conclusions on their own. The same narrative used to justify American involvement in Vietnam has been taken off the shelf, recycled, and is being used again to justify America's involvement in the Ukrainian conflict today. Sometimes, history both rhymes and repeats itself.

This author's particular concern is that much of the American public is being purposefully misinformed. They are being intentionally misled by many in government circles who project a false and dangerous narrative which only serves to feed Russia's paranoia against NATO and the West left over from the Cold War. This narrative also serves a dual purpose; it continues to inflame American opinion against anything Russian. It matters little if Russia's paranoia is based in fact or not. Russian reactions to oppose NATO expansion towards it borders can lead to a major nuclear world war. Since American foreign policy is often cloaked in subterfuge wrapping itself in the veneer of pursing an international equivalent of making the world safe for Democracy and maintaining the Roberts Rules of Order from the American perspective, the probability by the Russian side to miscalculate Western intentions and misstep in response are extremely high. Further, it inflames anti-American sentiment and resentment in other flashpoint regions, and notably this negative effect is especially true in the Middle East.

Americans are being fed a steady diet of daily government propaganda, flat out lies and misinformation regarding America's motives to intervene in the Ukrainian-Russian War. Unfortunately, many in the American press corps industry today align itself with officially stated government positions and interests. They ignore legitimate counter arguments and even censor facts that would undermine their truncated reporting. The American media are not engaging in the rigorous pursuit of truth that serious investigative reporting requires. Instead, they willingly regurgitate blatantly false and misleading facts that often originate from effective American and Ukrainian propaganda campaign designed to support the official government narrative to continue the war. And the American Deep State also purposefully influences the average American citizen by often misreporting the facts concerning unfolding events on the battlefield in Ukraine's favor. The first casualties of war are always truth and innocence.

For example, the current war in Ukraine is the largest military operation since WWII. This is an astonishing fact. The conflict has far-reaching current and future world-wide repercussions for America. Yet rarely is this largest military conflict since WWII adequately covered by most American media. The conflict often fails to be the lead story in major news outlets. Why? Certainly, this is another important question which deserves an honest answer. And part of the answer to this question is the desire by those yielding power in government circles to control the official narrative. There is a concerted effort by upper echelon governement agencies afoot to undermine honest media reporting of the largest storyline of the ongoing greatest military conflict to transpire in more than half a century.

This entanglement demonstrates a textbook example of a strong corroboration between government and the Fourth of State. The media, both right and left, CNN, and FOX, cheer-lead in unison to support America's military intervention in Ukraine. The narratives regarding the Ukrainian conflict on both sides of the political spectrum are almost indistinguishable. But this growing interlocking relationship between government and the Fourth of State is a dangerous development which threatens to undermine the well-being of a free democratic society. In the long run, Democracy cannot survive without truth-telling by a vigilant press. Challenges by the press which expose government corruption are necessary to combat government overreach. The freedom of the Press and Democracy itself is perhaps not as alive and well in the United States and well as many Americans believe.

The Fourth of State is a massive corporate behemoth. It is comprised of only a hand-full of powerful Mass media conglomerates which can control the content of the message to the masses. They decide what news stories "lead" and what news stories are not allowed to surface to see the light of day. Way too often in America, the masses are being programmed to ensure the continued support for ongoing interference in the internal affairs of other sovereign nations, propagating wars and projecting American military power abroad.

The media in America today are playing a leading role to support American interventionist policies overseas. When the press fails to challenge government policies then government power and control over its citizens naturally tend to increase.

The media does so by failing to rigorously question the use of force in America's continuous interventions overseas. It does so by constantly miscasting Russia in the role as the bad boy aggressor on the world's stage, driven in every instance by an evil intent to oppose the spread of Democracy and reconquer Eastern Europe. The press portrays American foreign policy decisions as justified while opposition from foreign nations is always portrayed to be on the wrong side of the issue. Tough questions are avoided: this failure to seek truth is especially true concerning America involvement in Ukraine.

This exemplifies how this American foreign policy has been so successfully employed without meaningful opposition. A very profitable and often incestuous relationship now exists between the government and Fourth of State. Over time, this cozy relationship has developed between American government and the press. It is also a dangerous relationship susceptible of censoring inconvenient truths. One must ponder whether Operation Mockingbird is still operational.[66] So what is the truth of the matter regarding Ukraine that Americans are not receiving from the influential Fourth of State?

SECTION TWO:

THE REALITY OF THE CONFLICT TODAY

Let us clear our minds from government misinformation, make an honest attempt to strip out bias, and disengage from inborn jingoistic tendencies. The US press-corps narratives run by the major news conglomerates including CNN, MSNBC, NBC, CBS, ABC, and FOX news are all misleading or false. Here are the hard FACTS on the ground regarding the state of military conflict in Ukraine—many of them hiding in plain sight:

CHAPTER SIX:

America's Total Economic Warfare Against Russia

The use of sanctions form an integral part of America's vast arsenal when dealing with nations the U.S. considers hostile towards its national interests.[67] Certainly, Russia tops America's list of countries that is experiencing the blunt end of the application of these sanctions with Iran running in a close second place.[68] The express purpose of these targeted sanctions is to deter or compel the nation sanctioned to act in American interests without having to resort to place boots on the ground and to avoid all out military conflict. Sanctions in the toolbox of American statecraft come in many variations namely, economic, financial, and sanctions imposed related to perceived violation of human rights.[69]

By far, America imposes sanctions against other nations far more frequently and severely than any other nation on the face of the earth. Currently, America is sanctioning more than twenty nations throughout the world.[70] It does so to punish these nations for engaging in policies and actions America deems contrary to the rules based international world order. After all, it is this rule based international order that has been designed largely by America.[71] The goal is always to move the recalcitrant nation in the direction to support American interests abroad. Whenever soft pressure proves ineffective to prod other nations in the direction American foreign policy maker's desire, hard ball pressure tactics by various American agencies usually follow.

The best example which demonstrates America's uses sanctions to effect regime change in the western hemisphere during the last seventy-five years or so is Cuba. When Fidel Castro seized power in Cuba in 1959, shortly thereafter, a vast array of sanctions against Cuba was implemented to overthrow the Fidel Castro regime.[72] Using economic sanctions, America imposed a complete embargo to isolate the island barring trade between Cuba and American companies.[73] This embargo was soon joined by many of its allies which had a devastating effect on the Cuban economy. The embargo caused immense suffering in the lives of the Cuban people bearing the full brunt by the effects from American policy hell-bent on preventing the spread of Communism in the Western Hemisphere.

Seventy years later, many of these sanctions remain in place. The domestic economy of Cuba is still in shambles today resembling an economy reminiscent of the throwback era in the late 1950's and early 1960's. Official government policy implemented during the Kennedy Administration also includes the Bay of Pigs fiasco and an unsuccessful attempt to assassinate Fidel Castro.[74] Whenever soft sanctions fail to achieve the desired outcome, American agencies often ups the ante and outright precipitates regime change. This includes staging domestic coups and assassination attempts against foreign actors. You see, America seeks to control most major political and economic events occurring within the Western Hemisphere. This is America's Manifest Destiny, so many Americans believe.

When the Soviet Union invaded Afghanistan in 1979, the Carter Administration acted quickly to enact a grain embargo in response.[75] However, sanctioning agricultural products had unintended consequences. America's farmers were no longer able to ship their valuable produce to Russia. In swift reaction to American sanctions, Russia rapidly developed stronger economic ties with Ukraine. In short, Russia began to import significant volumes of grain from Ukraine instead of from American farmers from the Midwest.[76] Economic ties between Russian and Ukraine flourished because of these sanctions while economic ties between Russia and American farmers languished. In a nutshell, these sanctions backfired much like the American imposed sanctions against Russia are backfiring today. In both instances American sanctions represents the classic act of shooting oneself in the foot with one's own gun.

When Venezuela, Libya, Nicaragua, Iraq, and Iran attempted to abandon the Petro-Dollar system and trade for oil it owned and pumped from its own soil to export to other nations in their own currencies, the U.S. imposed severe economic sanctions against every one of them. It instigated guerilla warfare between internal rival political factions, threatened or flat out invaded these noncomplying nations with its military. You get a picture of what is really going on.

The current rounds of sanctions imposed by America and its NATO allies against Russia after its incursion into Ukraine were designed to weaken Russia internally and to effect regime change.[77] Nothing has changed in this regard since the Cold War. American sanctions include a strict prohibition prohibiting the transfer or trade of military equipment and weaponry with Russia by any third party nation during the Ukrainian military conflict.[78] These sanctions are also denying Russian access to the international SWIFT system, freezing out Russia from the international banking settlement system in an attempt to ruin Russia's external trade with other nations and to wreak havoc to its domestic economy.[79] Since the war began in earnest in early 2022, thousands of American corporations have either curtailed or ceased doing business in Russia.[80] Altogether, American and the West has imposed nearly 300 various government economic sanctions against Russia.[81]

America is engaging in complete economic warfare against Russia. A large part of this activity includes ongoing attempts to crash Russia's domestic economy. This is an extremely dangerous development. Economic warfare too often leads to outright open conflict between competing nations attempting to control a finite universe of natural resources.

In hypocritical hubris, at the same time and in the same military conflict, America and NATO are dumping billions of dollars into the economy and flooding the conflict with lethal offensive weapons to enable Ukraine to sustain its fight against Russia. America and NATO can flood Ukraine with lethal weapons and provide it with a vast array of weaponry, but China, Iran, and any other ally of Russia cannot aid and/or support Russia in the same manner without experiencing the wrath of American imposed sanctions.

America excels in asymmetrical warfare. These intentional acts of economic warfare against other nations are highly effective. They strangle the adversary's domestic economy and break its will to effectively resist American power. In effect, they impose the classic siege to surround the nation, just like successful sieges occurred during military campaigns in the ancient world. The domestic economy is damaged, while the general population suffers from severe shortages in critical life sustaining goods and even faces starvation. The goal is the same whether occurring in ancient or in the modern era, to pressure the enemy into submission. More often than not, this strategy usually succeeds, with America gaining the upper hand over its opponent. It leads to a decisive victory without the need to employ major military assets. This strategy also significantly limits American military casualties.

America thru official diplomatic channels is also sending a strong blunt message to China. It is warning China against providing military arms and assistance either directly or covertly to Russia.[82] America is also signaling a willingness to punish China with trade restrictions in the event that China ignores these warnings or attempts to work around these sanctions and provide military aid to Russia.[83] Most recently, in typical gunboat diplomacy mode, America has orchestrated the largest naval exercises in decades in the South China Sea just off China's mainland, punctuating its warning to China not to assist Russia.[84] The American Navy is flexing its military muscle in China's own back yard for a reason. Of course, America and NATO exempt themselves from the sanctions it imposes on others while dumping billions of dollars in military supplies into Ukraine. Imagine the uproar in America that would break out if either Russia or China led full-scale naval exercises in either the Atlantic or Pacific Oceans directly off either American coastline. Imagine the response by America if Russia or China attempted to prevent military hardware transfers between America and its allies.

The message that America is conveying to China and the rest of the world is clear: America is the dominant hegemonic empire striding alone on top of the power structure of the world's pyramid. Do not challenge us and our allies. Do not test our interpretation and implementation of the international rules and order. Acquiesce to this strategic pecking order in the world, adopt American based policies, or there will be severe consequences imposed against your country. The rest of the world hears this message clearly and is increasingly appalled by these blatant acts of overt hostile intimidation.

The world is growing weary of America's continual meddling in their internal affairs. Nations are beginning to push back. The recent formation of the BRIC alliance, with other nations petitioning to join its ranks, is the direct result of American hegemonic mania gone wild. The entire continent of Africa is also resisting American sanctions and supports the Russian side in Ukraine. Most African nations today equate American foreign policy in the Ukrainian conflict with that of their historical experience when they suffered enormous loss at the hands of western colonialism.

The list of economic and other sanctions imposed against Russia is a long one. It includes the illegal confiscation of more than three-hundred and fifty billion dollars of Russian owned international central bank reserves, as well as the seizure of other privately owned Russian assets. This confiscation of sovereign bank reserves has never happened before—the U.S. Dollar reserve system has been weaponized against Russia.[85] Maintaining American hegemony, thru the U.S. dollar reserve currency system via exorbitant privilege is by far the major force driving U.S. foreign policy actions initiated in Ukraine as it is around the globe. If America were to lose its position as the keeper of the worlds' reserve currency and the Petro-Dollar framework finally collapses, America's ability to run large annual deficits to support its massive war machine and maintain its massive military footprint overseas would cease overnight. This of course is the sine qua non of America's involvement in Ukraine, as it is elsewhere.

However, a profoundly serious downside risk is involved when initiating economic conflict against one's competitors. The nation who attempts to game the system in their favor, maintain economic dominance or limit economic growth and trade, will often trigger a backlash against its actions. It often leads to military conflict between these same nations who are competing for economic supremacy. Both WWI and WWII offer prime examples of major military conflicts that were caused in this manner. They exacerbate existing tensions between already competing economic rivals. This same scenario is being played out again in former Soviet satellite nations and in Ukraine.

Prior to both WWI and II, the British Empire was facing challenges from an emergent Germany by its rapid growth and burgeoning economic might. The rapid growth of the German Navy challenged the supremacy of the British Navy in both the North Sea and in the Northern Atlantic Ocean.[86] This development threatened British shipping sea lanes. From the British point of view, the growing German naval threat and increasing maritime prowess had to be stopped. England is an island nation largely dependent on imports to maintain its economic strength. It could not risk allowing the German Navy to control the shipping lanes in the North Sea. Another prime example is the use of America imposed draconian sanctions against Japan prior to WWII preventing Japan's ability to import oil. This embargo suffocated Japan's domestic economy. Arguably, these sanctions were the final straw precipitating Japan's decision to attack American Naval forces at Pearl Harbor.

Yes, in like manner, America's decision to intervene in Ukraine by imposing significant economic and military sanctions against Russia significantly increases the chances to trigger WWIII. Wars are often caused by stoking fears of economic insecurities between competing nations. The current military conflict in Ukraine certainly fits the bill.

CHAPTER SEVEN:

Ukraine and NATO Expansion

In 2014, the Ukrainian military was in a pitiful condition largely unable to fend for itself. It was suffering from years of neglect and from chronic internal corruption. One military source even describes the condition of the Ukrainian military between the period from 1991-2014 as being decrepit.[87] It certainly was in no condition to stand up against Russia's superior armed forces. American government intelligence agencies saw this weakness and began building up the Ukrainian military. Considerable military aid and assistance were provided from the U.S.[88] As a result, the armed forces in Ukraine have become larger than military forces of Germany and France combined, with enhanced offensive capabilities.[89] Just before the current conflict with Russia began in earnest, the number of German and French ground forces combined totaled approximately 350,000 troops.[90] In comparison, Ukrainian forces were larger than most NATO nations with reserves numbering approximately, five hundred thousand (500,000).[91] In fact, next to Turkey, Ukraine has the second largest standing army in Europe.

In 2014, Russia's military was also in a weakened condition. It was unable to successfully mount long term military ventures beyond its own borders except for navigating through smaller regional conflicts.[92] Certainly, the condition of Russia's weak military forces posed no threat to NATO at that time. It must be asked, why was the build-up of these large Ukrainian military forces with substantial offensive capabilities necessary?

Since 2014, America rapidly escalated its arm shipments to Ukraine. It poured billions of dollars of military aid along with inserting additional military advisors and CIA operatives into the country.[93] Today, tens of thousands of Ukrainian forces are being trained to fight against Russian forces in U.S., England, and in Europe.[94] America's decade long meddling in the internal affairs of Ukraine and building its military infrastructure did not go unnoticed in top Russian government circles. They understand that ultimately Russia is the intended target in Ukraine's massive military buildup. Further, Russia certainly understands that Ukraine's overall militarization has been largely orchestrated by the Americans who have supplied massive amounts of aid and assistance. For more than a quarter century, America along with NATO, has been grooming Ukraine as well as other former Soviet satellite nations for membership into the EU and NATO. Had they not done so, Russia would not be able to persuasively argue that its military intervention in Ukraine was only for defensive purposes in response to aggressive NATO expansion.

Due to America's previous actions in the region, Russia had advance warning concerning the West's intentions towards Ukraine. In addition to Ukraine, early on, NATO targeted the nation of Georgia to flip into the Western orbit.[95] Georgia is in a nearby region lying between the Black and Caspian Seas directly on Russia's southern border. Georgia also borders both Turkey and Iran on its southern border. Strategically located, loaded with valuable minerals, and operating major oil pipelines connecting the Eurasian continents with one another, Georgia was the perfect location to initiate standard American foreign operating procedures against Russian regional interests. These oil pipelines supply millions of barrels of oil per day, generating billions of dollars for the Russian economy. Until 1991, these nations were part of the former Soviet Empire. Both Ukraine and Georgia are strategically important forming part of America's overall strategy to isolate and control Russian power and to deny Russian influence in the region.[96]

Since gaining independence from the Soviet orbit, Georgia, like its next-door neighbor Ukraine, became a leading recipient of U.S. foreign military aid.[97] There is evidence that powerfully connected players inside Georgia were covertly recruited by Western operatives to initiate a color revolution known as the "Rose Revolution" in November 2003 against the pro-Russian regime. Various alphabet agencies provided material support to advance American interests and depose President Eduard Shevardnadze, who previously had been a major part left over from the past Soviet regime in Georgia.[98] This meddling in Georgia's domestic elections successfully brought a pro-western regime with pro-western democratic reforms to Georgia. Additionally, NATO integration fulfilled American ambitions to move Georgia firmly into NATO's camp. It was an extremely successful undertaking by the West and Georgia remains a staunch NATO ally today.

Both the Rose Revolution in Georgia and the subsequent Euro-Maiden color Revolution in Ukraine successfully implemented regime change favorable to Western and especially American interests. What a remarkable coincidence. Naturally, the elite in charge in the West want you to believe that this push for domestic regime change and pivot toward Western interests in both Ukraine and Georgia was entirely organically grown. They want you to believe that this result occurred without outside interference or support from the West. The evidence however points otherwise. Years of Western meddling including the clever use of cover NGO entities supported by George Soros's backed financial organizations, as well as operatives on the ground acting together finally paid off, and Georgia was flipped into the Western orbit in 2003 away from Russian influence.[99]

The West has taken a victory lap. Georgia's large shift away from Russian influence has been declared to be a significant victory for Democracy in the region. Since then, the Georgian military has been entirely integrated into NATO's military structure to the complete consternation of Russia. American meddling in the internal affairs and elections in every other formerly Soviet satellite nation reflects the same aggressive pattern implemented by the West. Russia naturally views NATO's military injection into both Ukraine and Georgia as an attempt to encircle its southern flank. Certainly, to anyone other than an ideologically driven neocon, this activity represents a direct provocation against Russian interests. If one were walking inside the shoes of Russian leadership, they would naturally be inclined to draw the same conclusion.

Russia, in reaction to the West's meddling in Georgia's internal politics and election of a regime favorable to the West, intervened militarily in these provinces.[100] It assisted two breakaway areas in Georgia in 2008 known as Abkhazia and South Ossetia. Since then, Russia has maintained a military presence in these breakaway regions countering the West's frequent meddling in Georgia's domestic politics.[101] And Russia invaded both Crimea and Ukraine for the very same reasons. Nevertheless, with its typical spin, the American State Department and White House defines the Russian response to American covet activities near its borders as unprovoked naked Russian aggression. American elites always spin Russia as the aggressive evil villain.

There is a common thread that reveals Russia's motive for intervention in both Ukraine and Georgia. These regions have sizable ethnic Russian populations and both nations border Russia. In contrast, American interests in Ukraine and Georgia are negligible at best. This brings into question America's reason for being there in the first place since its interests cannot begin to compare in importance to Russian interests. Russian interests include maintaining a stable relationship with nations along its direct southern borders that include historical relationships and close ethnic ties. Of course, America loudly protests and condemns Russia's military incursion into both Georgia and Ukraine. Yet, in both instances, Russia was reacting against NATO's previous expansion towards its homeland.

However, America always doth protests too much—to borrow a much-quoted line from the Shakespearian play Hamlet. CIA agents as well as other alphabet agencies were already present in Georgia agitating for a complete regime change against Russian interests prior to direct Russian military intervention[102]. America always claims ownership of the moral high ground when operating in the arena of international affairs. America justifies its right to intervene in the internal affairs of other nations insisting that is only in response to actions and activities first initiated by various evil and nefarious adversaries. All this posturing is standard American modus operandi skullduggery America calls statecraft. However, most often hidden from the light of day, American selfish ulterior motives for aiding other nations are involved. Most often, previous American meddling have set in motion a series of events in these nations which causes other nations to undertake measures to counter American actions to begin with.

Notice the obvious pattern—It all begins with a carrot: America comes striding along knocking on the door of a targeted nation with numerous wonderful gifts in hand. This especially includes the promise to spread Democracy, capitalism, and provide economic assistance. And of course, part of the attractively wrapped package to entice acceptance and cooperation is the promise to provide military protection against adversaries both real and imagined. An open invitation with open arms is extended to join the white hat side of the Western military alliance. Everything comes wrapped in a perfectly tied bow. Yet somewhere down the road it often ends at the other end of a large stick when immense pressure is placed on this nation to support American interests in the world. Either follow America's lead or suffer the wrath of sanctions. This includes meddling in its internal policies and internal government functions, regime change, and when all else fails, face the possibility of flat-out military intervention by the American side.

The news media at home can be counted on to carry the bucket of water for the home team. During nightly newscasts, the American people are informed that these military interventions are necessary. American intervention must be taken to save that nation from the clutches of a psychopathic tyrant mistreating his subjects and for the sake of spreading Democracy around the world. This script, or some variation, always reads the same. President Putin is the latest example how this predictable fear-mongering misinformation campaign tactic is successfully employed largely for domestic consumption at home. Wrapping one's cause in the red, white, and blue furls of the American flag is an effective strategy government uses to garner support at home and to loosen the purse strings to continue military spending. This allows Congress to support endless military adventures and interventions overseas. It is part and parcel of a propaganda campaign all sides engage in to support the ongoing war effort.

Of course, the Russian Government, as well as Putin, understand how America plays this game of geopolitical four-dimensional chess. Putin regards all this positioning with considerable suspicion. He views them with hostile intent aimed directly at weakening, encircling, and stripping Russia of its natural resources. He understands that Russia's ability to influence and guide strategic interests in its own regional backyard is the real target.

There is a powerfully entrenched cadre at work burrowed deep inside the caverns in American Government. Yes, there is a Deep State in America. This shadowy arm of government maintains a strong bias against Russia left over from the vestiges of the Cold War. Let's just say that keeping the boogey man mantra alive that anything Russian is evil that must be defeated serves the interests in elite circles at the helm within American Government. Trillions of dollars are flowing into U.S. Military coffers, the defense industry, and end up lining politician pockets. Every one of them handsomely benefit from this largess as long as this false narrative is kept alive. It is instinctively understood that once this narrative is debunked, the gravy train will immediately stop running and the goods will no longer be delivered. In practice, the donor class is in control running the show and pulling the strings inside the Washington D.C. beltway.[103] This is especially true regarding foreign policy. Narrow interests act together to keep the dollars flowing in their direction while the interests of the average American citizen are most-often ignored.

President Eisenhower accurately coined the phrase the Military-Industrial Complex in 1961 during his farewell speech to the nation to identify this activity. He did so when transferring the power of the Presidency to John F. Kennedy.[104] Eisenhower accurately identified these powerful forces at work. He warned against the threat of their shadowy nature, lawless tactics, hidden off-the-books budget without accountability, and coercion constituting a threat to the very fabric of American Democracy.[105] A large part of this Military-Industrial Complex is comprised by alphabet agencies identified by their acronyms.

The CIA and other alphabet agencies operate from a secretive off-budget government pocketbook known as the Black Budget.[106] Government expenditures to these agencies are marked classified. Only select government officials and legislators who possess top secret clearances can access this information. In addition to foreign actors, this means that the American public are denied knowledge as to how, when, where, and with whom American agencies are conducting covert operations overseas. It is a system susceptible to rampant fraud and abuse.

All we know for sure is that the annual budget of the CIA and related agencies standing alone is larger than the entire annual military budget of Russia.[107] In fact, the off-the-books budget of the CIA is larger than the military budgets of more than approximately 175 out of 195 nations in the world combined.[108] Recent annual budgets of the CIA and related agencies currently excess sixty billion dollars. If its budget were placed alongside the annual military expenditures against all other of the world's nations for comparison, they would be ranked as the fourth largest military related budget in the world.[109]

These expenditures routinely fund America's clandestine activities and illegal escapades initiated in other nations all over the world. In addition to the budget of the CIA, America's annual military budget is by far the largest military budget in the world approaching one trillion dollars annually in outlays.[110] The military budgets of Russian and China run at a far distant second and third place.[111] The entire military budget of Russia in 2021 was approximately sixty-three billion dollars.[112] This annual military expenditure by Russia hardly indicates an intent to create the ability to assault nearby NATO nations. These off-the-books budget items of CIA origin often target, manipulate, and control preferred outcomes to Americas liking in the internal affairs of foreign governments. These off-budget expenditures often include attempts to rig foreign election results. Ukraine is a prime example of American foreign election rigging and represents the poster-child in U.S. meddling in foreign elections.

CHAPTER EIGHT:

America Has Meddled in Ukrainian Elections

America has a long-documented history of meddling in the internal affairs in foreign nations and interfering with outcomes in their major elections.[113] None other than the former head of the CIA, James Woolsey, candidly admits this. When sitting for a recent Fox News interview and asked directly if America interferes in foreign election, he stated, "Oh probably, but it was for the good of the system in order to prevent the communists from taking over."[114] A little further along in the same dialogue, Woolsey stated that American interference was "only for a very good cause and in the interest of democracy."[115] More recently, U.S. National security advisor to President Donald Trump, John Bolton, readily admitted that America outright engages in coups in foreign nations to overthrow governments identified as hostile to American interests.[116] A recent research paper written by Dovi Levin, documented at least eighty-one past attempts by various U.S. agencies to intervene in foreign electoral campaigns aimed at changing election results from 1946 thru the year 2000.[117] The number of elections America has, directly or indirectly, interfered with attempting to manipulate the outcome and advance its dominance in world affairs should shock the conscious of its citizens. Unfortunately, the average American cares little concerning foreign policy initiatives and pays scant attention to foreign affairs.

The same modus operandi is at play by America to ferment regime change in the former Soviet Satellite nations including Georgia and Ukraine. Alphabet and other government agencies, (CIA, NSA, DOD, DIA, Pentagon, State Dept. etc.) acted in concert to conduct covert operations which led to the removal of a democratically elected official (Viktor Yanukovych) in 2014.[118] Yanukovych was replaced by Arseniy Yatsenyuk, a politician Washington policy elites considered to be more favorable towards Western interests. It was widely known that Yatsenyuk supported Ukraine's political and economic movement away from Moscow. Yatsenyuk was aided in his improbable ascension to power in Ukraine thru a color revolution created during the Obama Administration known as the Euro-maiden Crisis.[119] Why? Because Yanukovych, who was Arseniy Yatsenyuk's predecessor, preferred to pursue the path and maintain a policy considered to be in Ukraine's best national interest. He preferred for Ukraine to remain a neutral country in the ongoing embittered rivalry between NATO, America, and Russia.[120]

In a landslide election in 2010, Yanukovych was democratically elected President in Ukraine by most of his countrymen.

However, his more nuanced political policies favored Russia.[121] This position ran afoul of American foreign interests in the region and especially impeded Ukraine's entry into the EU and NATO. American officials, especially U.S. Deputy Secretary of State Victoria Nuland and U.S. Ambassador Geoffry Pyatt, advanced the American position that Yanukovych needed to be replaced by someone with a pro-western stance.[122] And they set in motion covert activities to accomplish just that outcome. It simply did not matter that honest election results in Ukraine had already occurred that were more favorable to Russian interests.

As long as Yanukovych remained in power with the ability to guide Ukrainian politics, his more neutral policies were considered unacceptable to western elites who were certainly attempting to determine geopolitical interests in the region in America's favor.[123] When internal political turmoil erupted in Ukraine, which America strongly encouraged, Viktor Yanukovych feared for his life. He was forced from political office fleeing from the country for his safety.[124] Shortly thereafter and magically, back-to-back Yatsenyuk and Zelinsky regimes whose policies are far more favorable toward supporting western and especially American interests in Ukraine have emerged.

Yanukovych saw obvious dangers ahead. If Ukraine pursued any policy other than steering a steady course of neutrality the security of Ukraine would be placed at risk. His policy position attempted to avoid becoming embroiled in the ongoing conflict between two antagonist superpowers.[125] In hindsight, his policy stance for neutrality was spot on. His policy position was simply designed to enable Ukraine to successfully walk the tight rope between rival Russian and Western interests that would have brought about a far better outcome for the average Ukrainian citizen today than the ongoing destruction of their country. One can argue rather convincingly that U.S. meddling behind the scenes in the murky shadows in Ukraine's national elections led directly to the elections of pro-western presidents. This in turn has triggered a series of unfortunate events that has led to the current major military confrontation between Ukraine and Russia.[126] These dots aren't hard for anyone to connect. All one needs to do is open one's eyes to see the reality happening on the ground.

The Kremlin and Vladimir Putin are aware of America's covert interference during Ukraine's 2014 presidential election cycle. The perfectly timed visits by both Senator John McCain, as well as undersecretary of state, Victoria Nuland at the height of the Euro-Maiden crisis in 2014 magnify the extent of American intervention.[127] It outwardly signaled to Ukrainian citizens American displeasure against Yanukovych and his regime. American actions taken in support of political opposition overtly telegraphed America's firm support of the rebellion against him remaining in power. During this election cycle more than one hundred government police were massacred by violence encouraged by embedded Western spook agencies.[128] This activity certainly has CIA earmarks. These covert dealings led to the ouster of the pro-western leader Yanukovych. This violence against the democratically elected regime was all along encouraged by American covert acts.[129]

Imagine Russian's visceral contempt for these cloak and dagger machinations. And imagine Russia's elite watching now debunked allegations made over and over by American government officials alleging that Russia materially interfered in the last two U.S. Presidential elections. A large segment of the American media, as well as prominent members of Congress and even Presidential candidate Hillary Clinton repeatedly beat the drums of this false narrative in primetime American news media and on the Senate floor. They ranted incessantly against Russian espionage, painting Russia as an unscrupulous adversary that must be stopped. They dogmatically stated that the failure to act militarily against unprovoked Russian aggression threatens American security interests world-wide. They made these assertions as gospel truth without factual verifications. This false narrative has been so successful that a sizable percentage of Americans still believe it to be true. Yet, this narrative has been sheer gaslighting of Americans from the very beginning.

Can you visualize the message Russia's ruling elite are gleaming from witnessing these charades that are played repeatedly by American government agencies. One hand spread false claims accusing Russia of significant election interference in American 2016 and 2020 Presidential elections. The other hand actively guides American interference in the presidential elections in Russia's next door neighbors Georgia and Ukraine. The chutzpah of this underhandedness is off the charts. It was not very hard for Russia to draw the conclusion that both Ukraine and Georgia are installed American puppet regimes functioning as de facto NATO integrated nations. And it is not hard for Russia to imagine that it is the next target on America's list for regime change.

CHAPTER NINE:

Ukraine Is a De Facto NATO Nation

Ukraine is now fully dependent on American and NATO aid and military backing for its national survival. By every measure and metric, Ukraine is treated as a signatory member of NATO. Ukraine enjoys most of the benefit from military intervention on its behalf in accordance with Article Five of the NATO treaty without becoming an official charter member of NATO. Ukraine receives vast amounts of NATO, as well as American armaments and the training of its military by the Western Alliance. Without vast amounts of NATO and especially American assistance continually pouring across its borders and into its war chest, the war in Ukraine would have been lost to Russia a long time ago. Shades of South Vietnam are certainly noticeable here. In the end, the result of this conflict will be much the same for America. Without full mobilization, neither NATO nor America can match Russian combat troop strength on the ground, a prerequisite impeding any chance to expel Russia from Ukraine.

Currently, America is providing the bulk of Ukraine's annual military budget.[130] American and European humanitarian aid is all that is keeping the proverbial wolf from the door and Ukraine away from defeat and complete collapse. This aid pays the salaries of Ukrainian government workers, the military as well as their pensions.[131] In 2021, the entire Ukrainian military budget was approximately six billion.[132] Since this military conflict began in earnest in February 2022, America and NATO have ramped up its assistance supplying more than one hundred billion dollars in military and humanitarian support to Ukraine.[133] This amount is not a typo. This amount represents a fifteen-fold increase beyond Ukraine's annual military budget in place shortly before the conflict with Russia began.

The degree of American military support to Ukraine is staggering. It suggests that ulterior motives are at play other than making Ukraine safe for Democracy. This is especially the case when Americans are in desperate need of relief at home where too many veterans are penniless and homeless. Veterans live on side streets in squalor without financial assistance while the U.S. pays the weekly salaries of Ukrainian soldiers to fight against Russian soldiers thousands of miles away.

After this military conflict is over, in addition to more than one hundred billion dollars already provided, Ukraine will require massive amounts of financial aid to rebuild its shattered economy. Current cost estimates run as high as five hundred billion dollars to rebuild Ukraine, which is being destroyed from the ravages of war with Russia. Of course, if the West wins, America will kick in most of this aid, courtesy of the already beleaguered U.S. taxpayer. In this event, the total cost to the American taxpayer for intervening in this conflict could well exceed one trillion dollars.

Admittedly, a long list of nations receives and benefits from American Government aid and assistance. This foreign aid package usually includes protection monies against mutual foes. Actual promises and guarantees are usually made enabling these nations to rest safely under the protective umbrella of the U.S. military and shielded from its enemies. Prime examples of American aid and assistance first coming to mind include Western European nations after WWII via the Marshall Plan, as well as the original formation of NATO. Other prime examples of American foreign aid include South Korea, Taiwan, Saudi Arabia, and of course Israel. This represents the positive side of American foreign policy put in place more than half a century ago. However, the golden age of American altruism is well past.

There is also a negative side. Nations receiving American assistance soon awaken to the stark reality that noticeably short strings are usually attached to this generous foreign assistance. At some point in the future a quid pro quo will be required. It means that in exchange for the benefits received, a willingness to follow America's interests in the world is expected to be reciprocated. And often, American foreign policy objectives in the end, run counter to and inevitably are at odds with the national interests of these benefactor's as well as the wellbeing of its nation's citizens. Gifts from America often come in the guise of a trojan horse. This horse remains inactive until American foreign interests assert themselves, demands suddenly emerge, and pressure is applied to follow

America's lead in world affairs—or else. Ukraine is caught up in this power play and will continue to be ensnared in America's web of influence for the forseeable future.

CHAPTER TEN:

American Foreign Policy Is the Sine Qua Non of the Ukrainian Conflict.

Repeatedly, America's intervention in the affairs of other nations is cloaked in a clever guise that it is benevolently doing so to spread Democracy and actively oppose ongoing oppression perpetrated by evil regimes. After all, it is argued that American's simply should not stand idly by and watch a regime that brutally represses the rights and freedoms of its citizens without coming to their rescue. The rule of law and Democracy are at stake. The list of dictators America has labeled as evil and has removed or attempted to remove from power is quite lengthy: several attempts to assassinate Fidel Castro (Cuba, 1960-61); Joao Goulart (Brazil, 1964), General Ngo Dinh Diem (South Vietnam, 1963 assassination assisted by CIA), Manuel Noriega (Panama, 1989), Afghanistan (1979-1982), Serbia (1999), Nicolas Maduro (Venezuela, 2018), Saddam Hussein (Iraq, 2003), Muammar Gaddafi (Libya, 2011), Bashar al-Assad (Syria), Mohammad Mosaddeq (Iran, 1953), Yanukovych (Ukraine, 2014) plus the ongoing attempt at regime change in Iran.[134] And now none other than Vladimir Putin has been placed on America's updated removal from power list. This list is by no means an exhaustive one. It represents only the tip of the iceberg of continual American meddling in the foreign affairs in other nations during the last seventy-five years or so.

Wherever America interferes in the internal affairs of other nations, undue influence naturally develops, which inevitably favors American interests. And in the long run the assistance received comes at the expense of that nation's own interests. Sometime American assistance or interference causes long term economic damage, and even social collapse. Perfect examples of these horrendous outcomes occurring elsewhere include Cuba, Libya, Iraq, and most recently Afghanistan. Another example, American forces are occupying part of Syria, over its government's strong objections since September 2014. The CIA supplied opposition militias with military weapons and other assets on the ground to assist in the attempted overthrow of the Assad regime in Syria.[135] Although uninvited, American forces have remained in Syria now for more than eight years. This direct military activity inside Syria represents an undeclared war against the current Syrian regime. At other times, American agencies work behind the scenes to subvert and control the outcomes in major elections in other nations around the globe.

And make no mistake about this, America did interfere in Ukraine's national elections in 2014. The echo of this scenario should sound familiar. America's meddling in Ukraine's national election resulted in the election of a President and administration with a demonstrably pro-western stance. And it replaced a regime with a demonstrably pro-Russian stance. To this day, a heavy cloud of suspicion lingers over this leaning pro-western president's elections win.[136] Both President Yatsenyuk's and Zelensky's ascension to power in Ukraine since 2014 have resulted in a massive increase in Ukrainian military capabilities and Ukraine's de facto integration into NATO at the expense of its relationship with Russian and with other neighbors in the region.

Today, America provides the bulk of weaponry and military support to Ukraine.[137] America is injecting more than one hundred billion dollars to keep the ongoing conflict against Russian aggression from completely collapsing. Since February 24, 2022, America has also provided real time military intelligence from its satellites to Ukraine to identify, directly target, and destroy Russian forces.[138] There is hard evidence that America provided the real time intelligence to enable Ukraine to successfully sink Russia's major warship (the Moskva) in the Black Sea at the outset of the war.[139] Without American and NATO support, Ukraine would have been defeated militarily on the battlefield during the early stages of the war and this conflict would already be over. Of course, despite evidence to the contrary, Russia is repeatedly labeled as the aggressor in the Ukrainian conflict.

Susan Rice, national security advisor to former President Obama, states the American official position in Ukraine succinctly: "This is not about U.S. and Russia. This is about whether the people of Ukraine have the opportunity to fulfill their aspirations and be democratic and be part of Europe, which they choose to be."[140]

Notice the convenient use of the "straw man" argument. Russia doesn't object to Ukraine becoming a democratic nation or interfere with its desire to develop stronger trade ties with the West—only that Russia and Ukraine would continue their historically close relationship with each other[141] Further, America's involvement in shaping the outcome of Ukrainian elections in its favor in 2014 thru clandestine and manipulative means doesn't easily fit the definition that Ukraine is functioning as a democratic country does it. Notice America's hypocritical position—that it is the beacon of light actively spreading democracy throughout the world. Yet, American fingerprints are all over manipulating the voting results of foreign elections, including Ukraine, that overturns the will of the people in those nations. Apparently, people living in their own nation cannot be trusted to vote for pro-western candidates who favor democracy and simply are incapable of understanding the policies and supporting the politicians that are in their bests interests. It often becomes necessary for America to act proactively to ensure favorable results to its liking regardless of domestic impact. This illustrates Susan Rice's unique definition of democracy. Many Americans would not recognize or accept American interference in foreign elections if behind the scenes manipulations in other nations were revealed to them.

American past foreign policy initiatives have often supported many militant regimes both right- and left-wing dictators, and strong-armed hooligans. This list includes the likes of Mohammad Reza Shah Pahlavi, the Shah of Iran, Saddam Hussein of Iraq, and Pinochet in Chile[142] America has also supported the violent overthrow of democratically elected politicians to gain leverage in America's favor. And it can hardly be said that Ukraine resembles anything close to being governed by democratic rules or principles.

An extreme irony is at play here. Ukraine has been and remains one of the most corrupt nations on the face of the earth.[143] It possesses only a modicum of democratic features and largely reflects the oligarchic Russian characteristics with which it once was joined at the hip. Certainly, as most Americans understand the term, most key components which form the make-up of a democratic society are missing in Ukraine. Freedom of speech, freedom to worship freely, freedom to assemble peaceably, and freedom to petition against the government are freedoms that the Zelensky Ukrainian regime routinely represses.[144] In March 2022, Zelensky banned all political opposition groups that opposed Ukraine's official position of war with Russia operating against his policies.[145] And in 2023, Mr. Zelensky suspended Presidential elections altogether until the conflict with Russia is concluded.[146] How on earth can the American electorate continue to believe that Ukraine functions as a legitimate democracy instead of the corrupt oligarchy that it is defies rational thought and strains one's credulity.

The electorate are being misled by American government officials. A complicit media plays along to support the false narrative to convince a majority of the public that it is on the right side of history and pursuing a righteous cause to accomplish vital strategic objectives. In other words, America is the chosen one, asserting the mantel of American exceptionalism, destined to become the enforcer of liberal international standards and establish and defend the spread of Democracy around the world. Maintaining international standards of behavior between nations is necessary, but hiding beneath the veneer this is all about controlling outcomes in nations and forcing conformity to a westernized version of ongoing efforts to build an international New World Order. If Russia, or any other nation, challenges existing American hegemony or the establishment of this new world order, America MUST intervene to maintain established international law and uphold order. After all, who else but America has the military muscle and capability to do so. America's own acts of aggression to impose its own interests throughout the world are always downplayed. Lost in the shuffle is the fact that America often intervenes to orchestrate the outcome and is the initial aggressor in foreign affairs.

CHAPTER ELEVEN:

Is Russia the Aggressor?

The West accuses Russia of entering Crimea in 2014 and into Ukraine in 2022 militarily without cause or justification. Of course, Russia repeatedly is labeled as the aggressor. However, the Russian military has crossed over the border into Ukraine for at least three legitimate security interests.

First, Russia considers that a NATO nuclear armed military force positioned along its 1500-mile-long southern border with Ukraine both to be a provocation and an unacceptable threat. It believes that if this scenario were allowed to fully develop that it would constitute an existential threat to Russia's existence. This is the Russian equivalent to the Monroe Doctrine. Honestly ask yourself if American foreign policy would allow a hostile nation to challenge America by arming either Mexico or Canada in a similar manner. Of course, it wouldn't.

Second, since at least 2014, largely due to western assistance and strong encouragement, Ukraine has amassed a rather large military force capable of initiating offensive operations against Russia.[147] Large quantities of lethal U.S. military aid have poured into Ukraine from the West. A large contingent of American advisors including CIA operatives have also been on the ground in Ukraine. For more than a decade they have been training the Ukrainian military to counter Russian interests in the region.[148]

Additionally, since 2014 the Ukrainian government has repeatedly threatened to take back Crimea from the Russians by force.[149] In order to do so it amassed thousands of troops in Eastern Ukraine shortly before Putin decided to move troops into Ukraine in early 2022.[150] This is an important factor that is being completely ignored by the Western media. Ukraine was planning its own military incursion into Eastern Ukraine which would have led to the deaths of many ethnic Russians. Ukraine's control of Crimea would threaten Russian control of its strategic military base in Sevastopol. Ukraine also shut off a large portion of Crimea's water supply to civilians before Russia moved into Crimea.[151] The Ukrainian government passed legislation to prohibit the use of the Russian language in schools, government, and public discourse even though these areas in Ukraine have sizable Russian speaking minorities numbering in the millions.[152] Not to mention the fact that historically Crimea and Odessa have been largely Russian regions.

Coordinating closely with Western nations, Ukraine has attempted to isolate Crimea from the rest of the world to cause internal turmoil and to initiate economic collapse. The goal was to effect a change in government away from Russian influence favorable to the Ukrainian regime and the West.[153]

All of these coordinated efforts with American assistance certainly smack as intentional acts of provocation. In response to these acts, Russia intervened militarily in Crimea and among other steps constructed a long bridge to link Crimea with the mainland to circumvent Ukrainian/Western policies and prevent sanctions against Crimea from succeeding in crushing Crimea's economy.

The current military conflict between Russia and Ukraine officially began in February 2014 when Russian forces crossed over the Ukrainian border and seized control of Crimea.[154] Putin justifies his decision to initiate this military incursion into Crimea based upon witnessing a series of previous hostile acts taken by the American led NATO. He views NATO's ongoing expansion towards Russia in general, and NATO's agreement during an official Bucharest pronouncement in 2008, to integrate both Ukraine and Georgia into the EU and NATO, as a direct threat to Russian territorial sovereignty. The Russians argue that NATO's aggressive expansion policies have triggered their decision in 2014 to annex Crimea bringing it back into the Russian fold. Putin was also genuinely concerned regarding the safety of the lives of millions of ethnic Russians living in Crimea and in the Donbas Region in Ukraine. The history books are replete with brutalities perpetrated by both sides and certainly these past experiences cause angst in both Russia and Ukraine which affect policy decisions in both nations.

Further, the majority of Crimean's are ethnically Russian, not Ukrainian. This ratio of this ethnic mix is high and almost two-thirds of the population is ethnic Russian.[155] Russian immigration into the Crimean region and control goes back to the days of Catherine the Great more than 200 years ago.[156] Russia's historical ties in Ukraine are very old whereas

Ukraine's present-day borders were first drawn on a map on September 12, 1991. Ukraine, as it exists today, became an independently sovereign nation for the first time on this date.[157] Thus, it has only existed as an independent sovereign nation to control its own destiny for thirty-eight years. Prior to this time and for more than a hundred years, Ukraine was part of the now defunct Russian Empire.

Again, the historical backdrop to this conflict is never reported honestly by the western media. Yet, to understand the root causes of the current conflict grasping the historical backdrop in this region is critical. Only then can one become confident he is accurately judging which side is likely more justified in their actions than the other. There is an extensive history between the people in this region. Often, and for centuries, both sides have transgressed upon the rights and freedoms of the other. Bloodshed and seizing the spoils of war have often occurred on both sides for centuries.

American foreign policy completely ignores this historical reality. Instead, American interests are asserted in the region regardless of historical realities or the effect it has on the well-being of the population at large. In fact, American policy is downright hypocritical. Domestically, America jealously guards the rights of its minority population, even carving out preferential treatment for individuals with a legally designated minority status. However, when millions of ethnic Russians living in Ukraine are treated as second class citizens, and worse, not a whimper of empathy is extended towards this ethnic Russians population. Not a peep from the arch defenders of minority rights in American government can be heard. To the contrary, American foreign policy supports the oppressors who oppress Russian ethnic minorities. American foreign policy conveniently ignores the recent atrocities committed at the hands of the Ukrainian government against ethnic Russians living in Ukraine. It does so to accomplish its own selfish geopolitical objectives in the region. This is rank hypocrisy.

The debate concerning which side has caused the current conflict to erupt into open warfare represents the classic which comes first, the chicken or the egg enigma. There is certainly enough blame to go around. It cannot be denied however since the end of the first Cold War in 1991, NATO and the West have been the ones expanding toward Russia's borders and not vice versa. And it certainly cannot be denied that America spends almost twelve times as much on its military budget then Russia does. American military bases, not Russian, are strategically positioned throughout the globe. By far, America is far more aggressive in the world's affairs than Russia. This really is not even a close call.

Third, since at least 2014, at the direction of its government, Ukrainian military forces have constantly shelled the eastern regions of Ukraine.[158] The eastern regions have strong historical ties including linguistic and ethnic with strong leaning sympathies toward Russia. Due to these abusive policies backed by the Ukrainian government, four provinces—Luhansk, Donetsk, Zaporizhzhia, and Kherson—split from Ukraine in 2014 preferring instead to align with Russia. In fact, these regions voted overwhelmingly to align with Russia instead of Ukraine.[159] In retaliation, upwards of 14,000 civilians—mostly ethnic Russians living in Eastern Donbas region—have been slaughtered by the Ukrainian military and paramilitary forces between 2014 and 2022.[160] Many of these atrocities were carried out by the AZOZ battalions who harbor fascists Nazi leanings with Kiev's tacit blessings.[161]

The reality on the ground is that since at least 2014, Ukraine and Russia have been at war in the Donbas fully eight years before Russia's decision to invade Ukraine.[162] In fact, America has provided most of the military assistance to enable the Ukrainian military to do so. A compelling argument can be made that America was not only aware but encouraged Ukraine's military operations against the breakaway regions in Eastern Ukraine and Crimea resulting in thousands of civilian casualties. Ukraine justifies their military actions in the Donbas and in Crimea because these regions chose to rebel against harsh Ukrainian rule. But without American military aid and assistance, it is questionable whether Ukraine had the military capability to attempt to suppress the rebellion led by a sizable percentage of ethnic Russian citizens living in the Donbas. It was an internal civil war and should have remained so.

Also being ignored are the initial provocative acts taken by the Ukrainian government to strip ethnic Russians living in Ukraine of their rights, dignity, and even lives. Government passed edicts prohibiting ethnic Russians from speaking in their own ethnic language in public or passing their Russian heritage on to their children.[163] The West, led by the U.S., is not without fault in this conflict. It has exploited obvious historical cultural fault-lines in this region, some existing for centuries, to pursue its own selfish interests.

America's meddling in Eastern Europe has provoked Russia's current military incursion into Ukraine. The art of American statecraft is to initiate internal turmoil and conflict using subterfuge to initiate regime change. At the same time, run a misinformation campaign at home and abroad accusing the other side of doing precisely what your side is doing. It is an old Marxist ruse and, often, a highly effective one.

This is the favorite stratagem America routinely pulls from its toolbox of foreign policy options when operating abroad. It all begins when the CIA and other aligned operative agencies target a nation to prime the pump for regime change favorable to American interests. This includes positioning forces and increasing military presence nearby to isolate and surround the targeted nation. Sometimes just threatening to use force and playing the card of gunboat diplomacy is all that is needed to obtain the desired outcome. Contemporaneously there with, impose sanctions to weaken the nation's domestic economy. At the same time, select and groom local political candidates favorable to Western interests for ascension to power and control. In the shadows, provide ample amounts of cash and material support on the ground during the election cycle on behalf of the candidates America prefers. Finally, once the favored regime wins political office, continue to provide the puppet regime with financial support and military aid. This aid and financial assistance will continue to flow until the installed regime deviates from America's strategic interests. When this occurs, select, and groom the next regime, and hand pick candidates for installing the next American puppet. Wash, rinse, and repeat.

This two-pronged heavy-handed approach divulges standard American statecraft procedure in action. The entire process is designed to damage the domestic economy and stir up internal strife which increases internal instability and disaffection among that nation's citizens to effect regime change in America's favor. It is a phenomenally successful strategy that has been used over and over. And during the last half century, America has turned the implementation of this strategy from art into an exact science as it influences the results of government elections throughout the world.

America's track-record is excellent at destabilizing, deposing, and installing regimes favorable to American interests. The trouble with practicing American statecraft in this manner is that the nation being interfered with eventually wises up to America's machinations. It then reverts, often violently, to its historical roots. The prime example of this is Iran reverting to Islam after the western installed Shah of Iran was deposed by Ayatollah Khomeini in 1979.[164] Iran has been a treacherous adversary opposing American interests in the Middle East ever since. Long-term, America is alienating nations with its short-sided meddling schemes where American leaning regimes have been installed. As a result, the list of American Allies continues to shrink around the world.

Russia has often experienced firsthand the negative impact from these standard American statecraft practices. Even after the Cold War ended in 1991, Russia has been repeatedly sanctioned for various contrived reasons by America. At the same time, NATO has continued its march advancing eastward towards Russia's historic boundaries to surround and isolate Russia from the international community. American foreign policy vigorously pursues its aggressive policy to "westernize" nations on or near Russian borders. Both Ukraine and Georgia are prime examples of American statecraft in action.

One can certainly grasp how Russia perceives the implementation of continuous American sanctions targeted against it, as well as NATO'S relentless expansion towards its borders. The degree of paranoia this causes inside Kremlin walls regarding the West's true intentions is understandable. Adding fuel to the fire, NATO, America, and the West often inflames the Russian government by ignoring Russian concerns and blocking Russia's protestations at the United Nations and other international official forums designed to address these concerns. Psychological and Political warfare against Russia are additional tools in America's foreign policy toolbox uses with frequency. These tools are attempting to stymie Russian interests world-wide.

However, this time America's patented strategy to effect regime change appears to be backfiring. Unlike dozens of smaller nations that are easily bullied and pushed about by America, Russia is a much larger nation the U.S. has chosen to shove around. In land mass alone, Russia is twice the size of America. Russia has proven itself capable to handle the immense stress these sanctions cause. And Russia anticipated and has prepared well advance for America's standard ploys. So far, Russia has shown quite a remarkable resilience and ability to withstand American sanctions. This time, in its attempt to weaken Russia in Ukraine, America may have bitten off more than it can chew in its attempt to weaken and destabalize Russia.

CHAPTER TWELVE:

Ukraine Is Not Currently Functioning as A Democracy.

Ukraine currently functions under the jackboot heel from authoritarian lock-down one-party rule. President Zelensky came into power during the Trump Administration.[165] For the record, prior to his nomination for the Presidency in 2019, Ukraine's current leader Volodymyr Zelensky was a comedian. He won the highest political office in Ukraine without any government experience whatsoever.[166] During the election season, candidate Zelensky's major campaign promise he made to the Ukrainian voters was to avoid war with Russia and negotiate an end to the ongoing costly civil war in Ukraine.[167] And he won the election largely due to his promise to sit down across the table with the Russians and negotiate a settlement to restore peace. Unfortunately, like most politicians, his campaign promises were merely empty pledges made to secure votes and win the election. After winning the election in a landslide, Zelensky ignored his campaign pledges and instead pursued a completely opposite course of action leading to the current direct confrontation with Russia. Zelinsky's sudden change of direction in policy was fully encouraged and supported by various American government agencies. Of course, Zelensky received material support from various American sponsored agencies during his election campaign.[168] After his election, American aid has only increased.

Zelensky now governs Ukraine as an American puppet. He is holding onto power only because he is receiving vast amounts of ongoing direct American financial aid and military support. Wherever American foreign policy employs the carrot and stick approach over the policies of the regime, including Ukraine, American dominance in the country affairs usually results. Ukraine has proven that this time it is no different. This relationship meets the definition of being a puppet regime, i.e., one who acts at the direction of U.S. officials and dances to the tune of America's directives.

Currently, opposition political parties are outlawed by the Zelensky regime—they are illegal. Freedom of speech is heavily censured, and speech deemed to be against government policies is ruthlessly crushed.[169] Opposition to regime policies is squelched with dissidents suddenly disappearing from their homes and off the streets never to be seen again. Members of the Ukrainian government are assassinated whenever a slightly perceived deviation from official Ukrainian policy occurs.[170] President Zelensky has also accused the Russian Orthodox Church in Ukraine of sedition and of actively aiding Russia. His policies have closed the doors to most Russian Orthodox

Churches in Ukraine denying the Orthodox faithful full freedom to worship.[171] Hundreds of priests are under surveillance and dozens of bishops and priests have been placed under house arrest.[172] There is little doubt but that many Russian Orthodox priests and parishioners are sympathetic to and aligned with Russian policies. But the hallmark of authentic freedom is to allow opposition from competing voices to be heard and to challenge policies they disagree with. Freedom or religion and freedom to petition the government are fundamental rights found alive in any healthy democracy. But these fundamental democratic rights are being ruthlessly crushed by the Zelensky regime in power today.

Many Americans are unaware that not only is Ukraine undemocratic in practice, but, it is one of the most corrupt nations in Europe, if not the world.[173] It has become the world's black market sandbox enmeshed in illicit human trafficking, running weapon bio labs on behalf of western interests, money laundering for the world's uber-rich, and operating an open bazaar that sells military hardware to dangerous nations and groups.[174] Zelensky himself has become rich at the expense of his nation and its citizens.[175] Recently, it has come to light that Zelensky and his inner circle buddies are most likely skimming hundreds of millions of dollars off the top from US aid and financial assistance to line their pockets.[176] There is further evidence that in the middle of this conflict, his family recently purchased a villa in Egypt for millions of dollars.[177] This is hardly the right atmosphere that is conducive to sustain any semblance of generating viable democratic institutions.

Anyone who honestly believes that Ukraine is functioning as a free Democracy should instantly call into question one's credibility. Old men and young teenage boys are taken from public streets by force, conscripted into the military and with little training marched off to the front lines of the conflict.[178] Many of these young men will never return home again. They are hastily trained and then sent to the front lines. These ill prepared soldiers wind up being used as cannon fodder in the largest battle in the war known as the meat-grinder in Bakhmut and most recently Avdiivka where Russian forces enjoy a considerable advantage in airpower and artillery.

This is the stark reality of the state of Ukrainian Democracy. This is the basic nature of the regime that America and NATO enthusiastically support. This is the nation ruled by oligarchic overlords that America has hitched its wagon to. America uses a litmus test when implementing foreign policy. It is the bottom-line approach: whoever and whatever methods that can secure and maintain American hegemony world-wide are acceptable. This is Real-Politic American statecraft in action.

The official American version that it is supporting the growth of democracy to make the world a safer place is sheer subterfuge. America will support any regime—left, center, right, fascist, communist, noncommunist, pink, brown, green, purple—which stands the best chance to advance American interests in the world. This certainly has been a pragmatic approach. However, this underhandedness undermines fundamental American principles and beliefs. It also affronts the American value of authentic freedom and liberty. And it is unequivocally un-American.

CHAPTER THIRTEEN:

Ukraine Can NOT Win the War Against Russia Without Direct NATO Intervention.

It is a mythical contrivance that Ukraine can defeat superior Russian forces without NATO boots on the ground backed with NATO air support. Yet, senior ranking government officials and high-ranking military brass are constantly feeding this line to the American people.[179] The official American narrative played over and over is that Ukraine is winning and can win this military conflict. The standard U.S. position both President Biden and his Secretary of State, Anthony Blinken, spout off with regularity from their official government positions is that America will continue arming and supporting Ukraine for "as long as it takes" to enable Ukraine to expel the Russians from within its recently drawn borders.[180]

This official narrative also claims that the Ukrainian military will mount a successful counter-offensive to dislodge Russian forces from within Ukrainian borders. It is touted that Crimea will be retaken from the Russian occupiers. This bravado regurgitated by government officials, upper echelon military brass, and echo chambered constantly by western media is a pack of lies. It is sheer propaganda contrived to keep the arms flowing from America—in other words, to keep the gears turning in the military-industrial complex machine the mighty beast must be fed. And feeding this machine is devouring billions of dollars in U.S. tax-payer's money daily.

The mainstream media routinely peddles these noxious falsehoods. They tout that a Ukrainian victory and Russian defeat on the battlefield is just around the corner and a fait accompli. None other than the top U.S. General, Chairman of the Joint Chiefs of Staff, Milley recently reassured the American public during an interview that the Ukrainian military will achieve victory against the Russians.[181] More recently, President Joe Biden during his speech at the NATO Summit in Helsinki on July 13, 2023, declared that Russia has "already lost the war".[182] President Biden is either intentionally lying, being deceived by his deep state advisors, or he is delusional. The author's best guess is that a mixture of all three is involved.

However, the reality on the battlefield is much different. Russian casualties are reported with artificially inflated body counts while Ukrainian war casualties, that are easily more obtainable by our side, are not being reported at all. For more than a year Americans have also been told that the Russians are running out of live ammunition. Yet, Russian the artillery barrage all along the 160-mile battle-front only continues to intensify.[183] It is Ukraine and the West, not Russia, that is running out of artillery shells and manpower.

More importantly, unless NATO directly intervenes, Ukraine CANNOT win the war against Russia. This is the fatal flaw in America's policy decision to militarily arm Ukraine. Since WWII, America often intervenes in military conflicts without clear objectives or with any definite end point in view. This half-measured approach without clear up-front goals to achieve clearly defined objectives has been disastrous for American interests abroad.

Russia enjoys both strategic and tactical advantages on the battlefield. These advantages are proving to be almost insurmountable. Russian dominant military strength in Ukraine is considerable, including a vast numerical superiority in artillery, manpower, and a superior integrated air defense system. Russia's air force dominates most interactions with Ukraine's depleted air force over the skies in the Ukrainian conflict.[184] The Ukrainian Navy on the Black Sea has been neutralized and except for an occasional noteworthy strike ceases to have meaningful impact.[185] In other words, Ukraine has no Air Force or Navy to speak of, with an inability to counter Russian forces in these critical areas of military power that are necessary military components to achieve victory.

In the air, on the land, and in the sea, Russia has the upper hand. Russian forces also enjoy an exceptionally large logistical advantage against NATO since the conflict is playing out near its borders in its own backyard. America and NATO simply are not supplying the advanced weaponry, advanced aircraft, and long-range missiles necessary to enable the Ukrainian military to succeed against the onslaught of superior Russian military forces.

Unless NATO is willing to provide upgraded military hardware and commit to introducing its own troops on the ground, this conflict will end in a humiliating Ukrainian defeat. In fact, contrary to the BS spin that is commonly broadcast by western media, Ukraine is suffering overwhelming losses on the ground and a catastrophic downturn in its economy.[186] Yet the lapdog Western press repeatedly and dutifully reports that Ukraine is winning the conflict. It is even far more farcical to suggest that Ukraine can defeat Russia or regain major territory lost east of the Dnieper River, including Crimea without direct NATO intervention.

Actual body counts of dead and wounded Ukrainian soldiers don't lie. Rough estimates show that the Ukrainian military lost between 150,000-200,000 of its most seasoned military personnel during the first year of the war. There are predictably another 100,000 personnel that have been wounded.[187] These casualties represent an exceedingly high percentage of Ukraine's original active fighting force. Reserves numbering another 250,000 shortly before the conflict in early 2022 are also being depleted at an alarming rate. A large majority of the Ukrainian original fighting force has already been decimated from the overwhelming advantage in Russian firepower. In some quarters, Ukrainian estimates of losses of boots on the ground exceed 400,000.[188] To put the extent of these horrific losses on the battlefield in perspective, American total combat losses during the entire Vietnam War were 58,220.[189] And American casualties during WWII totaled approximately 420,000. When this conflict ends, Ukraine will sustain a higher casualty count than America did during WWII.

On the front line Russian forces enjoy an extreme advantage by a ratio of ten to one in artillery over Ukrainian forces. This advantage simply cannot be overcome by the Ukrainians themselves.[190] Further, it is unsound military doctrine to mount a counter-offensive capable to expel Russian forces from its borders like Ukraine recently attempted to do without the assistance from close air support. Sending Ukrainian ground forces into combat without supplying sufficient air support simply represent a death sentence for many unfortunate Ukrainian soldiers. Once they are transported to the front lines, the life span of many Ukrainian soldiers can be measured in minutes, hours, and days.

Domestically, Ukraine's infrastructure is being systematically reduced to rubble. A continuous bombardment from accurate Russian munitions hammers away at strategic targets throughout Ukraine. Major cities in Eastern Ukraine are completely depopulated. Ukraine is being depopulated by both mass emigration as well as catastrophic losses of its young men and women on the battlefield. Between eight and twelve million of its citizens, which represents one third of their entire population, have fled from their homes to neighboring countries, many will never return.[191] At war's end, it is possible that Ukraine will suffer almost one million casualties when wounded are included in the count. At times, almost forty percent of the electricity and water in Ukraine is inoperable.[192]

Twenty percent of Ukrainian territory in the East—the most industrialized and agriculturally productive—is in control of Russian troops.[193] Russian forces have also gained control of the largest nuclear power plant in Europe. Ukrainian GDP has fallen by almost thirty-five percent with almost $500 Billion of its material and infrastructure damaged.[194] After the conflict ends, Ukraine will require massive amounts of foreign aid and assistance to rebuild the infrastructure of its war-torn country. The cost of this aid will be second in magnitude only to the Marshall Plan implemented and funded by America to rebuild Europe after WWII. Only thru artful deception perpetrated on a gullible American public by the lap dog media can one believe that Ukraine is winning or able to win this war. It is institutionally dishonest to suggest that Ukraine is holding its own against Russian forces or capable of winning this conflagration without direct NATO intervention.

In stark contrast, Russia is suffering virtually no material damage to its domestic infrastructure. It's GDP has fallen by less-than five percent and Russia's currency the Ruble at times has maintained and even gained in value.[195] Russian losses in military personnel during the first twelve months are more accurately estimated at less than 100,000.[196] Of course, American official sources dishonestly tout significantly higher Russian casualties. However, the numbers game the government plays with the U.S. general population mirrors the misreported body count of dead North Viet Cong soldiers inflated during the Vietnam War. Both Ukrainian and American estimates of Russian losses on the battlefield are part of a coordinated misinformation campaign designed to keep military aid flowing from the west and the conflict against Russia continuing to roll. This also helps keep negotiations to end the conflict from occurring. These grim factual statistics conveniently go unreported in the West.

Notably, at least in the short run, the United States seems to be the one nation that is benefiting from the Ukrainian conflict. Ukraine's future looks bleak. It may end up in a downward spiral unable to recover going the way Iraq has since U.S. intervention across its borders during the Gulf War. However, in the long run, the U.S. will also pay a very heavy price for intervening in Ukraine.

CHAPTER FOURTEEN:

Why Negotiations Are Evasive

Russia describes its military invasion into Ukraine as a *special military operation*. An official declaration of war has not been made.[197] From the onset, Russia's military incursion into Ukraine has attempted to limit the war to a regional conflict to prevent escalation and avoid a direct conflict with NATO. In other words, Russia is intentionally attempting to achieve its military and political goals at the lowest level of war possible and keep the war as local as possible.

Contrary to inaccurate American media reports concerning Russian original intentions, the best evidence supports the position that Russia initiated its military operation in Ukraine in an attempt to negotiate a truce to prevent further NATO expansion. Previous efforts to negotiate a settlement with the

West without military involvement had fallen on deaf ears. This explains why the Russian initial invasion was purposefully limited in scope and breadth. It was calculated to finally catch the West's attention and bring it immediately to the negotiating table. It was intended to be a cold bucket in the face of Western leaders.

But when Russian forces crossed the Ukrainian border, America and NATO unexpectedly refused to negotiate. Unfortunately, NATO's reaction to Russia's initial incursion was to up the ante and flood Ukraine with massive military aid and assistance. Russia now has no other alternative than to create the buffer zone in Ukraine by force. Most likely, when the dust finally settles on the battlefield, Ukraine at best will become a neutered nation whether the West and NATO like it or not. And in the event the city of Odessa falls into Russian hands, Ukraine may cease to exist as a viable country. Its ability to export products cheaply on the Black Sea will simply cease to exist.

In fact, Russia's original goal was not to conquer and occupy all of Ukraine. How do we know this? Simple logic tells us. The number of Russian military and logistical support personnel initially entering Ukraine in 2022 was around 100,000 to 125,000 soldiers.[198] This number of Russian military personnel crossing the border is insufficient to defeat the numerically superior Ukrainian armed forces entrenched around Kiev, Ukraine's capitol city. Certainly, Russia's original invading forces were inadequate in number to occupy and control the entire land mass comprising Ukraine which is equivalent to the size of Texas. Russia was forced to call up an additional three hundred thousand men and women from its military reserves once America and NATO showed little interest in negotiating a settlement and instead signaled a resolve to continue the conflict.[199]

Instead, a more reasoned analysis leads to the conclusion that Russia entered Ukraine and took control of the Donbas region by force to protect the lives of ethnic Russians living in Eastern Ukraine including Crimea and to prevent further NATO expansion.[200] The Russians desired to trigger negotiations which would lead to a final solution and not to engage NATO in direct military conflict.

However, now there are too many casualties on the battlefield. There is simply too much at stake for Russia to allow Ukraine and the West to win. Russia will not stop the conflict until it accomplishes its objectives. Further, Russia will not accept a stalemate akin to the negotiations which ended the Korean War. There will not be a 38th parallel line drawn in Ukraine. This is what makes the Ukrainian conflict so dangerous. The likelihood that this conflict will end in a stalemate is a delusional fantasy the West can only wish for. Russia simply holds the upper hand on the battlefield and will not allow a stalemate to develop.[201] America and NATO would need to risk WWIII to change this outcome.

Putin is pragmatic. He certainly understands the reality that Russian control of Ukraine would require an extremely large occupational force sufficient in number to operate successfully in a hostile environment. We are talking upwards of the continual presence of 500,000 trained military personnel on the ground, sufficient in force to subdue the Ukrainian population for many years. This number of forces would involve fifty percent of its current standing Army. This scenario is unrealistic, and Russian leaders know this.

Putin also understands all too well that any Russian occupational force would be confronted by a hostile native population. These citizens would be all too willing to engage in a campaign of constant guerilla warfare to dislodge Russian forces from the Ukrainian homeland. Putin and other politburo members experienced firsthand the affairs of the former Soviet Union and are painfully aware of the magnitude of resources that were necessary to maintain control over the former satellite Warsaw Pact nations. It was a fool's errand then and would be a fool's errand in Ukraine now. Russia wants no part in this scenario to become an occupational force again. Furthermore, Russia is no longer interested in spreading Communism throughout the world. The utopian dream of a world controlled by communist ideology died in the rubble along with the collapsing concrete structure from the fall of the Iron Curtain in the 1990's.

However, American propagandists continue spinning outlandish claims that Russia is seeking to return to its former glory days anxious to rebuild a new revitalized Soviet Empire. A favorite kin nard broadcast frequently by western new outlets is that Russia is planning to reestablish the Soviet Empire to reclaim control of its former satellite nations. So, the argument goes, often reported during the Vietnam era, if America and NATO allow Ukraine to be defeated and fall back into the Russian orbit, Poland and Romania and the Baltic Nations will become Russia's next prime targets. This is the commonly heard narrative heard from America's political class by both the left and right side of the isle in Congress. It is the now debunked Domino theory being played over again.

In fact, this narrative was prevalent among Republican hopefuls participating in the first televised Presidential debate held by FOX news. This chronicle of events is utter nonsense—Russia wants nothing of the sort. Russia has learned valuable lessons from its experiences in its former satellite countries during the Cold War, as well as its more recent misadventure into Afghanistan, that American leadership has yet to grasp. Overall, Empires costs enormous sums of dollars. They divert enormous amounts of capital from productive domestic endeavors and place tremendous burdens on domestic resources. Burdensome taxes become necessary and politicians clamor for Central Banks, or the FED just prints the money to paper over the gaping holes in the budget to pay for endless conflict. As a result, inflationary forces usually take hold during military conflicts. This devastates the purchasing power of the domestic currency, often resulting in the impoverishment of its citizens. Eventually, in the end all empires decay and collapse from the increased weight of these extra burdens. The American Empire will not be the exception. You can safely place your bet on this outcome. However, be sure to take your winnings in gold and silver and not from depreciating U.S. currency.

CHAPTER FIFTEEN:

Russia Has Gained Significant International Support

American influence in the world is waning. As usual, western media is not informing its citizens concerning this rapidly developing state of affairs. A sure telltale sign of America's decline is reflected by the fact that many of the world's nations have decided not to support NATO's war against Ukraine. More than 150 nations have refused to join the coalition or supported Western sanctions. Instead, many prefer to maintain their trade relationships with Russia.[202] This includes most nations in Asia, the Middle East, Africa, and South America. Even NATO members, Hungary, and Serbia, do not fully support current sanctions against Russia.[203] Two other western aligned nations, Switzerland and Austria are refusing to join in many of the current sanctions imposed against Russia and are declining to confiscate Russian financial assets. They have made it clear that to do so is contrary to their national constitutions. Instead, Switzerland and Austria have pledged to remain neutral declining to provide offensive weapons in the conflict.[204] Turkey also is playing its usual game of politics and straddles the fence between Russia and the West. The world's two most populous nations with more than two billion people, China and India, have significantly increased their economic ties with Russia, a clear rebuke to American policy objectives and hegemony.

There are also signs that Europe is beginning to wake up from its self-imposed stupor to question its lockstep alignment with American foreign policy interests. From the start, America has placed pressure on its European allies to sanction Russia and extend the duration of the war in Ukraine. However, massive demonstrations against the war have broken out across major cities in Europe. Tens of thousands of Western Europeans have taken to the streets in their capitols to protest becoming more entangled in the Russian-Ukrainian conflict.[205] Due to Western imposed sanctions, largely demanded by American leadership, the economies in Europe are beginning to teeter into recession. Germany is nearing a deep recession. Yet, these large demonstrations in Europe against NATO's involvement in Ukraine are noticeably absent from most western media reports. Americans do not see the well-organized protests overseas dissenting against the ongoing war. These protests are simply being censored wholescale by the American news media.[206]

Most damaging of all, for the first time the U.S. dollar reserve currency system is being successfully challenged. An alternate system initiated by China, Russia, and other BRIC countries is being rolled out to replace the current American controlled system. Both Russia and China are busy amassing large gold reserves to support this new monetary system. Russia and China realize that time is on their side as America's national debt continues to spiral out of control. Both nations realize that at some future date, America's indebtedness will act to curb its ability to project military power overseas. And both China and Russia are also significantly increasing their military capabilities and expanding the size of their forces in anticipation of major open conflict with America and the West. Russia in fact is busy doubling the size of its military forces and capabilities in the event of war with NATO. Both Russia and China are in advanced stages of preparing for WWIII.[207] There could hardly be a more negative consequence for the West going forward due to America's decision to intervene in Ukraine. A major world war at this juncture would bankrupt the West.

It is perhaps the greatest foreign policy blunder to occur in more than a century to impose economic sanctions against Russia and China. The weaponization of the U.S. Dollar against Russia has become a fatal policy error. The net effect of these misguided policies has provided China and Russia with a strong incentive and rallying point to unite against a common enemy, an otherwise improbable military alignment. Historically, Russia and China are wary of one another. Certainly, they are not natural allies.

China obviously sees that a golden opportunity has emerged from American military intervention in Ukraine. China has decided that the opportunity is too alluring to ignore and wants to take advantage. China is not only securing vital natural resources from Russia at a cheaper cost but is spreading its influence and rapidly increasing its prominence throughout the Middle East and Africa. China is now challenging the U.S. dominance on the world stage since America's attention is clearly distracted elsewhere. Taiwan is in Chinese gunsights. Russia is backstopping Chinese ambitions with its potent nuclear arsenal as well as a large Navy with vastly greater ocean-going capabilities which complement nicely with Chinese naval forces. American military assets are stretched thin around the world and being challenged on multiple fronts. This international development represents a significant check against American hegemony.

Other nations in the world are taking note. They are keenly aware that a substantial geopolitical shift in power and realignment is rapidly taking shape. As a result, nations are beginning to realign their allegiances. The winds of change are shifting decidedly against American interests. Momentum is building in nations, including America's direct neighbor to the south, Mexico, to join the other side and abandon the U.S. dollar. The global south, including the entire African Continent is also signaling a willingness to join this fresh global movement to abandon the U.S. Petro dollar financial system. This international framework has been solidly in place since the Bretton Woods Summit in the aftermath of WWII. The common euphemism used to identify this ongoing movement against the dollar is de-dollarization. The breadth of this movement is international in scope and the speed of its implementation is accelerating. Ironically, American foreign policy has been a major catalyst undermining its own national interests.

Forty nations have already applied to become members of the recently formed BRIC alliance.[208] Six of these nations joined the BRIC alliance on January 01,2024—Saudi Arabia, Iran, Ethiopia, Egypt, Argentina, and the UAE.[209] This alternative financial system is designed to provide an alternative method to settle international trade transactions in currencies other than in U.S. denominated dollars. The implementation of this new international financial arrangement is further along than most living in the West realize.

The days of the U.S. Petro-dollar system and American control over the world reserve currency are ending. The stark reality is that America faces a financial crisis unable to afford to continue to act as the worlds lone Hegemonic Empire. It has become an Empire of debt consuming itself in a state of constant warfare. Most of America's military interventions overseas since WWII were unnecessary. America's unbridled ambition to maintain its position as the world's only hegemonic superpower has become its Achilles heel. Without changing course, America's decline will continue to accelerate, and in the end will destroy itself from within as all empires eventually do.

CHAPTER SIXTEEN:

American Hegemonic Interests Impede Diplomacy to End the Ukrainian Conflict.

Most shocking of all, powerful elites who formulate foreign policy in the underbelly within the American State Department and the environs inside other government agencies have taken negotiations to end this costly war off the table.[210] Many policy elites and think-tanks acting in coordination with the high-ranking American government officials believe that initiating a proxy war in Ukraine presents a win-win policy for American foreign interests. They believe that bleeding out the Russian military at the expense of Ukrainian soldier lives today saves the lives of U.S. military soldiers on the ground overseas in the long run. They also believe that weakening Russia and effecting regime change in Russia to dethrone Putin from power are legitimate American foreign policy goals.[211]

To accomplish these ends, America with NATO in tow, continues to pour massive amount of weapons and aid into Ukraine. But this activity by the West will only prolong the conflict. Of course, gauging this conflict from strictly the American vantage point that prolonging the conflict is part of an overall American strategy to weaken Russia, then it can be argued that the objective of the Ukrainian conflict is succeeding. However, a very good counter argument can be made that the opposite effect is occurring; European economies are weakening largely due to sanctions imposed against Russia. Further, Russia's military is arguably stronger today than before the war. Since the war began in 2022, trade between the EU and Russia has fallen by approximately eighty percent.[212] But America seems to be only interested in weakening Russia and dethroning Putin from power.[213] American foreign policy has been attempting to destabilize the former Soviet Union, and now Russia, since the beginning of the Cold War in the 1950s.

Yet at least some of the leaders in the Western European capitals are beginning to awaken to the reality that European and American interests may be at odds in the ongoing Ukrainian conflict. The longer the Ukrainian conflict drags on, the longer European economies will continue to weaken. This effect is already taking hold in Germany, Europe's premier industrial powerhouse. Western Europe is being de-industrialized. Behind the scenes, cracks in the NATO alliance are beginning to form. These cracks are undoubtedly widening and will become open fissures once it becomes apparent that Russia is gaining the upper hand and will win the Ukrainian conflict. At this point, a divergence between American and European geopolitical interests should continue to increase.

At the beginning of the conflict, Germany intentionally withdrew from a mutually advantageous economic relationship and abandoned its lucrative ties with Russia after American diplomats pressured it to do so. This economic relationship existing between Western Europe and Russia was solidly in place before the conflict began. Russia is a nation rich in mineral resources. It especially possesses an abundance of oil and gas which Western European nations need to supply its manufacturing base. Germany has historically deep economic ties with Russia. Germany possesses a mature manufacturing base in desperate need of raw materials from Russia and, at least until the current conflict erupted in 2022, Russia desired to sell its oil, gas, and other mineral resources to Western Europe, and especially Germany. It was a perfect match and a strong economic bond that mutually benefited both nations. Unfortunately, Western sanctions have backfired, and Western European economies are experiencing many long-term negative repercussions as a result. Paradoxically, the Russian economy is benefiting from NATO initiated sanctions.[214]

Russian economic relationships have pivoted away from Europe to Asia and Africa. To maintain the strength and growth of their domestic economy, the Russians are now successfully building economic ties with China, India, and elsewhere in the global south. Russia is abandoning its economic ties with Western Europe. Going forward, this process is beginning to undermine the vitality of European economies as Russia realigns itself with the East and Global South. Of course, American global corporations are anxiously standing by to fill the void left by Russia's exit.

This is a very significant development which is resulting from the Ukrainian conflict. Europe has forfeited a major strategic trading partner that willingly supplied it with raw resources at advantageous prices critical to maintaining its industrial base. Europe has managed to damage its relationship with Russia, perhaps irretrievably.

Unfortunately, most European governments, especially their top leadership, in their haste have overlooked this outcome and joined sanctions driven largely by American self-obsessed interests. Certainly, European nations are not benefiting either economically or militarily from western sanctions against Russia. The opposite is true. And unless Russia attacks a NATO nation, there are no benefits whatsoever for Western European nations to alienate Russia. Yet, a Russian invasion into NATO countries is very unlikely. Another unfortunate outcome of the war is that Russia, a historically Western nation with many historical links to the West, thru misguided policies, may have been pushed away from the West for good. The potential for Russia to serve as a natural valuable strategic ally against China to counterbalance Chinese ambitions in the region has been needlessly squandered. America has committed a colossal geopolitical mistake. Additionally, many valuable and strategic resources will flow east and south to China and India instead of to the West.

Western European government leaders should have pushed harder to resist American arm-twisting. They should have withstood American pressure and united to encourage negotiations to reach a reasonable compromise with Russia when the first salvo was fired in the conflict in early 2022. But American foreign policy pushed hard in the opposite direction to extend the war. American and European Union elites opposed negotiations and compromise with Russia.[215] This decision is driven by greed, outright hubris, and power lust that only benefits a tiny few. And American led sanctions are materially damaging the economies of its European allies.

Primarily this military conflict is NOT about enforcing a strategy designed to stop Russian aggression and preserving democracy in Ukraine. This result is secondary in importance to American real interests in the region. Although contrary to the official American position so eloquently stated by Susan Rice, this seemingly harsh accusation against America's officially stated position is nonetheless true. American foreign policy doesn't give a rat's behind about its official pronouncements that it is acting only to preserve Ukrainian Democracy and Ukraine's right to self-determination. This diatribe serves merely as a smokescreen for the masses to ingest and mask America's real selfishly driven geo-political interests in the region.

Unfortunately, Ukraine has become yet another American proxy pawn that is being used to further America's own strategic interests. It is the latest nation to be caught up in a series of America's ambitious overseas interventions. Ukraine joins this growing list of nations directly impacted by American military interventions since 2000: Iraq, Syria, Somalia, Libya, Yemen, and Afghanistan. If you can, please identify which of these nations have benefited from the dalliances of American military intervention into their nations. And please identify the names of any neighboring countries bearing the burden of receiving the throngs of mass immigration streaming across their borders who have gained anything due to warfare precipitated by inerrant American foreign policy, which triggered these mass migrations to begin with. European nations have been flooded by waves of mass migration of peoples from the Middle East and Ukraine largely due to America's meddling in the affairs of these regions.

Ukraine is being systemically dismantled by the superior might of the Russian military. American foreign policy machinations have largely caused this travesty to unfold. Its unstated goals: to utilize Ukraine to weaken Russia, undermine Putin, prohibit strong economic ties between Russia and the EU, hinder the development of China's silt road initiative, and control the vast Russian economic resources and assets, lies behind these unannounced objectives.[216] This is a rather long list of reasons. Added together, they accurately identify American real interests and motives behind its decision to intervene in Ukraine. It has little to do with preserving Ukrainian territorial integrity and supporting Ukrainian democracy.

Former U.S. National Security Advisor during the Carter Administration, Zbigniew Brzezinski, long ago succinctly sums up the underling basis of American position regarding Ukraine. In 1994 he stated, "It cannot be stressed strongly enough that without Ukraine, Russia ceases to be an empire, but with Ukraine subordinated, Russia automatically becomes an empire."[217] The Brezinski doctrine exposes what America's real objectives in Ukraine really are. That is, to undermine Russian interests at every turn and neuter Russia's ability to become an empire capable of competing against American interests. America is seeking to control governments and natural resources located throughout Eastern Europe and Central Asia five thousand miles away from its shores.

This underlying strategy lies at the heart of American foreign policy in Eastern Europe and Central Asia. America does not want Russia to become a competing empire with the ability to trade on par with itself in European and Asian nations. Even the remote possibility that Russia and Germany could unite again economically and militarily freaks out the American foreign policy establishment. Instead, America, with NATO tagging along, desires to control entry and exit from both the Baltic and Black Seas corridors for both economic and military reasons and to obstruct the Russian Navy's abilities from projecting its potent naval power in the event of war. And America desires to lock down its dominant trade position with the EU in place of the obvious alternative competing power, Russia. As has been allegedly quipped regarding the Water Gate scandal, "just follow the money."[218] Following the dollar trail leads directly to the unstated but real U.S. policy objective to feed the voracious appetite of the hydra-headed monster that defines American hegemony.

For American geopolitical interests overseas, there is a lot more at stake in Ukraine than at first meets the eye. Unless Russia is willing to accept Ukraine as a newly admitted and heavily armed NATO nation with a documented history of hostility towards ethnic Russians on its southern border, it is being left with little choice. Either Russia can allow Ukraine to be armed by the West and concede that it will join NATO; or it can decide to exercise the military option after diplomacy obviously failed to stop NATO's expansion east and neutralize Ukraine as a military threat. Russian leadership was not left with much of a choice. America, on the other hand, may eventually fall victim to its own flawed foreign policies. In the end, America geopolitical interests may be irreparably damaged due the strengthening ties between Russian, Chinese, the growth of BRICS and the birth of a new international monetary system.

CHAPTER SEVENTEEN:

Ukraine Is Not Vietnam— It Is More Dangerous

Unlike the Vietnam conflict, where North Vietnam and South Vietnam were smaller nonnuclear nation proxies aided by larger military powers pulling on the strings of its proxy states in the background, Russia itself is directly engaged in open warfare against America and NATO. Bluntly stated, two major nuclear powers are now directly confronting one another head-to-head. This is a direct military confrontation between armed nuclear superpowers. And the longer the conflict drags on, the more likely that one side or the other will miscalculate, misstep, and the war will escalate into a full-blown world-wide war.

Militarily speaking, the Ukrainian conflict is more like the Cuban Missile crisis in 1962 than any previous confrontation since WWII. Fortunately for all living today, the major difference is that the Cuban Missile Crisis never turned into an actual military conflict. Direct military confrontation between superpowers was averted. No bullets whistled through the air aimed at the mortal flesh of the enemy, fatal artillery fire was not exchanged, and both sides rapidly disengaged from the other to deescalate the conflict and prevent triggering a catastrophic world war. In fact, and repeated for emphasis, the Ukrainian conflict is the largest and most dangerous military conflict to break out on the world stage since WWII.

How will this conflict end?

Realistically, Russia has only two plausible options. It can surrender on the battlefield retreating in ignominious defeat with its tail wagging between its legs and run back to the confines within its own borders. This option, however, yields complete victory to American hegemony and kowtows to American and NATO interests. This choice allows Ukraine to turn into a heavily armed NATO nation with offensive capabilities positioned directly on the doorstep of Russia's southern border. This option also places the heartland of Russia and Putin's job security at significant risk. Finally, this option places Russia's only military seaport, Sevastopol, and its ability to control the sea lanes in the Black Sea at risk. Or Russia can bomb Ukraine back into the stone-age, demilitarize Ukraine, and strip it of any military abilities to attack Mother Russia in the future.

Not surprisingly, Russia has chosen to execute the latter option. In hindsight, it was a colossal American foreign policy error and gross miscalculation by its Department of Defense, State Department, and other involved U.S. government agencies to believe that Russia was too weak to resist NATO encroachment directly on its borders or allow Ukraine to join NATO under any circumstances. Further, Russia will never willingly allow the Black Sea to become a NATO controlled lake. There is simply too much strategically at stake for Russia to allow these potential outcomes to occur.

Unfortunately for both Ukraine and Europe, America remains laser focused on its attempt to accomplish its goal to weaken Russia and gain economic dominance and control over Eastern and Central Europe, as well as other Asian nations. To achieve this intended result America <u>continues to escalate</u> all phases of war against Russia. Instead of sending diplomatic signals to encourage negotiations and engage in a reasonable settlement, the message being delivered from the West to Russia is we will defeat you, Putin must be dethroned, Ukraine will win, and Russia will be forced to pay war reparations.

America has again recently escalated the conflict. It has done so thru its decision to deliver HIMAR'S, Patriot Missile systems, Bradley Infantry fighting vehicles, and now M1 Abram Tanks into Ukraine.[219] The next step will be to send advanced F16 fighter jets and other advanced weaponry into the conflict, a decision now being actively debated by NATO and the West.[220] Moscow is witnessing these decisions in real time and is receiving NATO's message loud and clear—Russia must either match the collective West's escalation of the conflict in Ukraine or risk losing the war. Russia has already calculated that it can ill afford to lose this conflict. At least on the Russian side, the decision to continue the fight is predictable. And Russia will match and escalate as required to achieve its stated goals. Even if it ends in WWIII.

American foreign policy is incoherent and has boxed itself into a corner. It must either concede that Russia will eventually win this military conflict or continue to escalate and pray that Russia blinks first. America is playing a strategic game of chicken. It is betting that it can control the outcome on the ground in Ukraine without precipitating WWIII. Washington DC understands that unless America and NATO, oops I mean Ukraine, wins this war against Russia, Russia will be the one dictating the terms and conditions regarding Ukraine's future. America wants to prolong the war until it can accomplish its unstated but real strategic objectives in the region. Russia will certainly oblige and double down in its efforts to win the conflict.

There is a third option available, the Dr. Strangelove option. America can continue its surreal geo-political waltz with the gods of war tempting fate and decide to escalate the conflict. They can do so by delivering F-16 fighter jets, advanced longer-range weaponry, (i.e., ATACMS) that can reach Crimea and deep inside Russian borders all the way to Moscow. The final step would be to introduce NATO ground troops, probably Polish and Romanian, into Ukraine. This is the next step in progression in the ongoing game of military escalation. This course of action is the preferred direction spooks at Langley and neo-cons wet dream about.

Only thru escalating the scope and scale of this military conflict does the West stand any chance whatsoever to negotiate a brokered peace favorable to Ukraine. However, upping the ante certainly risks triggering an all-out WWIII, if not Armageddon. Why not roll the dice—right? Go for it! Call Russia's bluff as many diehard neo cons who have President Biden's ear behind the curtains so to speak continue to advocate. What can possibly go wrong!

But what if Russia doesn't blink?

Certainly, to reverse the current course that is careening towards WWIII, an urgent U-turn by government leaders on all sides is needed. If a moment of sanity would occupy the interior spaces inside the dense skulls of American and NATO leaders, a real statesman would emerge and act rationally to end this conflict. Sober diplomacy requires the creation of an off-ramp for both sides to traverse. No stone would be left unturned to avoid the horrors of war that World War III would foist upon humanity. All available avenues to avoid a catastrophic world war between the world's two largest nuclear powers capable of ending all life on earth would be attempted. Backroom channel diplomatic signals would be sent to Russia to deescalate the conflict, come to the negotiation table and to reach a diplomatic solution to avoid a slight miscalculation that could trigger World War III. The game being played to expand American hegemony would at least be delayed. This approach should have already been initiated to prevent the escalation of this conflict into a major world war.

This is the rational diplomatic response Putin anticipated from the West. When Russian leadership in Moscow huddled together to formulate its policy and decided to launch its military campaign in Ukraine, it didn't dawn on them that the West would not immediately agree to sit down at the bargaining table to hammer out a settlement to end this long running festering conflict. When Russian government finally made the decision to push its military forces across the Ukrainian border in early 2022, the West's response led by American interests was not rational and not as Russia's policy elite anticipated.[221] The Russians were taken completely by surprise by the West's response.

Unfortunately, the opposite response occurred. Negotiations between Ukraine and Russia with Turkey acting as mediator in the spring of 2022 were squelched. After a month or so of negotiations, the two sides hammered out a tentative agreement to end the conflict in early April.[222] However, this negotiated settlement was not conducive to American real interests and actual goals in the region. This act to suppress meaningful negotiations to end this conflict early on, speaks volumes and exposes the West's true malevolent intentions towards Russia. Both sides have unfortunately gravely miscalculated the other's response to Russia's incursion leading the world headlong into a nightmarish WWIII scenario.

During the 1962 Cuban Missile Crisis rational diplomacy transpired on both sides to resolve that conflict, and this sober-minded approach is desperately needed today. This is the last time a similar historical event occurred that two nuclear armed superpowers collided head-to-head with each other on the world stage. During that crucial time, nuclear war was averted thru the courageous efforts by statesmen on both sides intentionally employing emergency diplomatic efforts to end the conflict.

President Kennedy and Soviet Premier Nikita Khrushchev opened direct dialogue with the other to avoid a direct military conflict.[223] President Kennedy withstood immense pressures from many of his advisors in the entrenched military establishment of his day to engage Russia in brinksmanship egging Kennedy on to escalate the crisis. Like today, too many of President Kennedy's advisors were all too willing to risk the possibility of precipitating all out Nuclear War. And like the Cuban Missile Crisis, the world again finds itself at two minutes till midnight. But Joe Biden is no John F. Kennedy, not by a long shot.

A rational diplomatic response by the West in Ukraine requires acknowledging that Russia has <u>legitimate</u> security concerns in its own backyard. It requires high level diplomats who are willing to signal de-escalation, not escalation towards Russia. It requires acknowledgement by America that its motives in this conflict are candidly driven by selfish and quite dangerous ambitions to assert American interests in Eastern Europe thousands of miles from its shores and diminish Russian interests. Finally, it requires an American President with his mental faculties fully intact who is capable of grasping the immense gravity of the situation which the world has blundered into. Is anyone confident concerning the outcome in Ukraine?

This time, the outcome in the current major conflict may be entirely different than the crisis from 1962. Intentionally or not, American foreign policy has recreated another Cuban missile crisis but with a perverse twist: America and Russia are now playing reversed roles. The irony is almost inconceivable. This time, America has advanced rather aggressively into Russia's backyard as Russia advanced into America's backyard almost seventy years ago in Cuba. This time, with few, if any, statesmen at the helm in the West, a direct war between major armed nuclear powers could become a hellish reality. This time, it will be America and not Russia who should blink. Otherwise, we are staring into the abyss of WWIII and nuclear war.

EPILOGUE

The current Ukrainian conflict is a watershed moment in world history. Looking back a few decades from now, many historians will identify this conflict as the seminal event that triggered a momentous rebalancing of the worlds' geopolitical structure. Major new alliances are forming and current relationships between nations are strengthening, especially between Russia and China, and weakening between the U.S. and Saudi Arabia. Only a few years ago it was inconceivable that this tectonic shift in power could become remotely possible. The strategic balance of power between nations and major regions of the world is significantly shifting. It is even conceivable that NATO itself may not survive intact. One of the major consequences of this war may be that NATO will unravel and begin to fragment into separate alliances.

Long term, unless America deviates from pursuing its position as world's sole hegemonic superpower, American and European interests will increasingly diverge, and NATO may cease to exist in its current form. Perhaps more ominous, if America stays on course and determined to remain as the world's sole hegemony, Russian and Chinese interests will continue to converge to prevent this outcome from occurring. Sooner, rather than later, there will be a significant high noon show-down between the West and East with Russia joining China in a major confrontation to determine the geo-political landscape of the world in the decades ahead.

Economic dominance as well as the military balance of power of nations is also shifting throughout the world. Especially noticeable is the shift in economic and military power away from the West towards the East along with the increasing inability of America to influence the outcome of major events in world affairs. This tectonic shift in power among the world's major powers with different ethnic, religious, and cultural roots is occurring for the first time perhaps in five hundred years or so. A key metric which signals this historic movement is the colossal transfer and accumulation of gold reserves by both China and Russia. Both nations as well as others are abandoning the Petro-Dollar fiat currency system in favor of an international monetary system backed by gold, oil, and other tangible resources.[224]

China is ascending as a major hegemonic power. However, the opposite is happening to the American Empire that finds itself rapidly descending in both power and influence. Joining together, Russia and China acting in concert are economic and military juggernauts capable of challenging and overtaking America's current position to act as the world's current sole hegemony.

It's entirely probable that other nations will begin to shift allegiances away from America once the winning side in this international struggle for dominance becomes apparent. The entire continent of Africa is already beginning to shift allegiances from the West to the East and join the BRIC's alliance of nations. The Middle Eastern nations of Saudi Arabia, Iran, and UAE have just joined the movement towards this developing economic powerhouse. Only a few years ago, it was inconceivable that American foreign policy would risk alienating Saudi Arabia and jeopardize its key role in support of the U.S. Petro Dollar system. Virtually every nation that has historically experienced the sting of American sanctions is highly incentivized to join the growing list of nations that are dumping fiat U.S. Dollars, abandoning the Bretton Woods System, and moving into a financial system backed by gold, oil, and other hard commodities.

Additionally, the dominate strength of the U.S. Dollar exists only thru its ability to control the world's reserve currency system. But this framework is beginning to unravel. This system is unwinding far faster than most experts have predicted. Few Americans understand what this development portends for them going forward. There will be severe consequences for American's financial interests' both domestically and internationally. Americans may soon wake up to find that the average American standard of living is beginning to resemble those living in substandard conditions existing throughout the impoverished third world. The American Empire is showing obvious signs of fatigue, exhaustion, and significant decline. For decades, America has overextended itself both at home and abroad. This accumulating national debt is an albatross around the neck of the nation choking off economic growth. This predicament will finally manifest itself and do severe damage to the American economy. The bill to be paid will finally come due.

America's dominant position as the world's premier superpower can only be maintained by its ability to run massive annual budget deficits. But the accumulation of astronomical amounts of debt required to feed a bloated bureaucracy as well as feeding its behemoth industrial-military complex is becoming mathematically impossible. This system literally operates as a massive Ponzi scheme. It is being financed thru a complex maze overseen by the U.S. Federal Reserve system. Behind the opaque curtains at the Federal Reserve, financial wizards are frantically mixing this magical elixir in their fantastical money machine which creates money out of thin air. This is the only force which keeps the gears in the system turning and prevents America's Empire of Debt from imploding. But America is now rapidly running out of runway.

America's large military footprint is currently entrenched throughout the world in more than eighty nations.[225] Maintaining this status quo is extremely expensive and can only be sustained by possessing a strong industrial and manufacturing base—an attribute America no longer possesses. Unwittingly, dismantled thru past policies by incompetent government administrations, America's once world class dominant manufacturing base has been allowed to slip away overseas. The American industrial-military complex now rests on a flimsy foundation of rapidly accumulating debt.

The catalyst that is accelerating this historic shift in the world's geopolitical structure is the military conflict in Ukraine. The odds are good that America's led proxy, Ukraine, will fail in its mission to defeat Russia and expel it from its borders. Almost immediately, America's prestige and hegemonic position in the world will become greatly diminished. The days the American Empire and America's ability to maintain and project its massive military footprint, power, and control over other nations are now numbered in years and not decades. By necessity, the current military number of military bases overseas will shrink with proportionate loss of American control and influence. Other nations will rapidly act to fill the void left by America's retrenchment.

The first Cuban Missile Crisis playing out over a period of thirteen days in October 1962, was also a major international event with consequences reaching far beyond the event itself. America prevailed in this confrontation by staring down the only other significant nuclear power of that era, the Soviet Empire, to become the world's only hegemonic superpower. This generally defined time frame from 1962 to 2000 represents the apex of the American Empire. Its position striding on top of the pyramid of the world's dominant powers has remained intact—until now. Americans today live in the twilight of the shadow of the American Empire feasting from the accumulated wealth derived from its past industrialized might and the affluence created by the hard work from previous generations.

But America is well into consuming its seed corn. Increasingly, the American economy is dependent upon borrowing from future generations and accumulating unsustainable debt. Russian, China, as well as a host of other nations including Iran and North Korea are aware of America's dire economic predicament and are now positioning themselves to challenge America's dominant position to act as the world's sole hegemonic power. They are aware that time is on their side. The clock is ticking as they say. America can expect increased challenges from its adversaries abroad going forward. This upshot is already evident in the Middle East.

The current standoff between Russia and America is a comparable major international crisis. Both international incidents involve the same two nuclear powers vying with the other for world dominance and control. However, there is one major difference between these two major historic events—the emergence of China. China is an ascendant global hegemonic power—especially a power to be reckoned with in Taiwan, the nearby China Sea, the Pacific Ocean, as well as the continent of Asia. And China has decided to side with Russia in this international conflict.

Today, the roles Russia and America are playing in this conflict are completely reversed. After the collapse of the Soviet Union in 1991, America adopted a foreign policy to intentionally drive NATO expansion eastward protruding into the underbelly and onto Russia's doorstep—despite repeated warnings by Russia for more than a decade—and especially warning America, not to do so. Russia on the other hand is claiming a flagrant violation to its rightful sphere of influence and security interests in this Eastern European and central Asian region lying next to its border. Russia alleges that NATO's expansion on its Southern border presents a considerable existential threat to its continued existence and rightful position among top-tier nations. The Russians assert that the West has crossed the <u>red line</u> it has warned the West for decades not to cross. Ukraine now plays the role of a proxy state on behalf of the U.S., which Cuba played as a proxy nation on behalf of the Soviet Union during the Cuban missile crisis nearly seventy years ago.

Unfortunately, this time the genie of military conquest cannot as easily be put back in the bottle. The consequences of this major military conflagration will be with the U.S. and the world for a very long time. Unlike the first Cuban missile crisis, when Presidents Kennedy and Khrushchev cooperated to diffuse the military conflict before it began, this time considerable warfare has already occurred between two of the world's major superpowers. Hundreds of thousands of lives have already been sacrificed on America's hegemonic alter that increasingly demands continuous warefare to sustain its bloodlust for power and control.

The Ukrainian military conflict is America's second Cuban missile crisis—only this time the ramifications are much more serious. Ukraine will soon join a long list of American proxy nations caught in the undertow of a dying American empire. Geopolitical realignment of nations is already well under way. These realignments will intensify and continue to undermine to finally bring an end to American Hegemony.

Pray that one side comes to its senses, backs off, takes an off ramp, and a compromise each side can stomach can still be reached. Otherwise, the world's elites may have managed to stumble into yet another World War. Poke an angry Bear and you can get mauled.

Endnotes

1 https://www.cnn.com/2023/04/04/europe/finland-joins-nato-intl/index.html/

2 https://dailyhodl.com/2023/04/26/us-dollar-suffering-stunning-collapse-losing-reserve-status-due-to currency-weaponization-report/ There are literally hundreds if not thousands of similar articles.

3 https://www.nato.int/cps/en/natohq/topics_192648.htm/

4 https://www.defensepriorities.org/explainers/the-futility-of-us-military-aid-and-nato-aspirations-for-ukraine/

5 https://www.foreignaffairs.com/russian-federation/world-putin-wants-fiona-hill-angela-stent/

6 https://quincyinst.org/report/the-dominance-dilemma-the-american-approach-to-nato-and-its-future/

7 https://www.vox.com/2014/9/3/18088560/ukraine-everything-you-need-to-know/

8 Population of Crimea: www.crimeahistroy.org: Most major Ukrainian cities have a sizeable ethnic Russian minority population.

9 How the war in Ukraine started by Eric Zuesse: (2019) The Liberty Beacon. There is evidence that American foreign policy was attempting to turn Crimea and Sevastopol into an American naval base to control the Black Sea.

10 https://www.npr.
org/2014/04/11/301749068/a-trip-into-odessas-rich-dark-history/

11 Id: See endnote #4.

12 https://www.encyclopediaofukraine.com/display.asp?linkpath=pag-es%5CS%5CO%5CSovietArmy.htm/

13 Ukraine's Nazi problem is real, even if Putin's denazification claim isn't" Politics & Policy (March 05, 2022)

14 The "Holocaust by Bullets" in Ukraine By Jennifer Popowycz, PhD. (January 24, 2022)

15 Mapping Militant Organizations. "Azoz Movement" Stanford University http://cisac,fsi.stanford.edu/mapping militants/profiles/azov-battalion

16 Monuments to Stepan Bandera: Wikipedia

17 https://historynewsnetwork.org/article/122778/

18 https://amgreatness.com/2022/11/18/its-time-to-speak-the-truth-about-ukraine/

19 https://www.e-ir.info/2015/03/10/ethnic-and-social-composition-of-ukraines-regions-and-voting-patterns/

20 https://greece.mfa.gov.ua/en/news/22578-pres-reliz-ukrajina-u-drugij-svitovij-vijni-1939-1945-roku/

21 https://www.e-ir.info/2015/03/10/ethnic-and-social-composition-of-ukraines-regions-and-voting-patterns/

22 https://www.vox.com/2014/9/3/18088560/ukraine-everything-you-need-to-know/

23 https://www.cfr.org/backgrounder/ukraine-conflict-crossroads-europe-and-russia/

24 The U/S. Decision to enlarge NATO by James M. GoldGeier, Brookings Review Brookings Review George Washington University/ Summer 1999.

25 Finland is the last nation to JOIN NATO in March 2023 principally due to the Ukrainian military conflict.

26 https://www.nato.int/cps/en/natolive/official_texts_8443.htm/

27 https://www.jstor.org/stable/2704032

28 https://www.theguardian.com/world/2021/nov/04/ex-nato-head-says-putin-wanted-to-join-alliance-early-on-in-his-rule/

29 https://www.cfr.org/event/role-nato-enlargement-revisited/

30 What Gorbachev Heard The George Washington University (December 12, 2017) http://archive/. gwu.edu

31 https://nsarchive.gwu.edu/brief-ing-book/russia-programs/2017-12-12/nato-expansion-what-gorbachev-heard-western-leaders-early/

32 From the time the Soviet Empire collapsed in 1991, high ranking American officials including the architect of American Post War foreign Policy have repeatedly warned against NATO'S expansion East. See comments by George E. Kennan, architect of America's post war strategy to contain the Soviet Union (February 07, 1997); See also The U.S. decision to enlarge NATO by James E. Goldgeier, Brookings Review (George Washington University/ Summer 1999).

33 https://sputnikglobe.com/20230210/putins-2007-munich-speech-stark-prophecy-or-reasonable-warning-that-fell-on-deaf-ears-1107315834.html/

34 Latvia, Estonia, and Lithuania do border Russia, but their size makes them inconsequential to Russian security unlike Ukraine which is larger than the state of Texas.

35 Ken Moskowitz, Did NATO Expansion really cause Putin's Invasion? The Foreign Service Journal (October, 2022).

36 Russia will act if NATO countries cross Ukraine "Red Lines" Vladimir Putin November 2021 Andrew Roth

37 John Meersheimer, University of Chicago, Sergey V. Lavrov Minister of Foreign Affairs, United Nations.

38 Global Times December 12, 2021 (http://globaltimes.cn/opinion)

39 https://scheerpost.com/2023/01/08/ patrick-lawrence-europe-and-the-legitimization-of-deception/

40 Mearsheimer, J. J. (2014). Why the Ukraine Crisis Is the West's Fault: The Liberal Delusions That Provoked Putin. *Foreign Affairs,* 93(5), 77–89. http://www.jstor.org/stable/24483306/

41 Until 2023, Finland was a non-NATO nation. Russia and Finland enjoyed a peaceful coexistence along a 1340 kilometer border without any incursions or major issues between them since 1989.

42 https://www.hi-us.org/ukraine-bombing-shelling-populated-areas-cause-incredible-suffering-civilians/

43 Why NATO has become a flashpoint with Russia in Ukraine// Counsel on Foreign Relations, January 20, 2022.

44 https://history.state.gov/milestones/1945-1952/nato/

45 https://www.nato.int/cps/en/natohq/topics_110496.htm/

46 Ibid: See endnote above.

47 https://www.cia.gov/readingroom/docs/STUDIES%20IN%20 INTELLIGENCE%20NAZI%20-%20RELATED%20ARTICLES_0015. pdf/

48 https://mronline.org/2022/09/14/ukraine/

49 https://ua.usembassy.gov/fact-sheet-u-s-nato-efforts-support-nato-partners-including-georgia-ukraine-moldova/

50 This is the Mackinder theorem. His belief that whoever controls the heartland in Europe and Asia, can dominate the geopolitical landscape of the world is still a prevalent view today.

51 https://oec.world/en/profile/bilateral-country/usa/partner/ukr/

52 https://www.history.com/news/ukraine-timeline-invasions/

53 https://www.atlanticcouncil.org/blogs/ukrainealert/putins-new-ukraine-essay-reflects-imperial-ambitions/

54 https://www.csis.org/analysis/update-forced-displacement-around-ukraine/

55 https://www.britannica.com/place/Ukraine/Soviet-Ukraine-in-the-postwar-period/

56 https://www.odysseytraveller.com/articles/history-of-ukraine-since-world-war-two/

57 https://www.wilsoncenter.org/event/25-years-independence-the-ukrainian-referendum/

58 https://www.nationalww2museum.org/students-teachers/student-resources/research-starters/research-starters-worldwide-deaths-world-war/

59 https://www.history.com/topics/vietnam-war/pentagon-papers/

60 https://www.nytimes.com/2023/06/16/us/daniel-ellsberg-dead.html/

61 https://en.wikipedia.org/wiki/Pentagon_Papers/

62 Id: See endnote #59.

63 Wikipedia: Pentagon Papers

64 https://www.crisisgroup.org/europe-central-asia/russiaus/saying-quiet-part-out-loud-russias-new-vision-taking-wes/

65 https://medium.com/insurge-intelligence/army-study-us-strategy-to-dethrone-putin-for-oil-pipelines-might-provoke-ww3-9b1d9dbe-6be9/

66 https://www.carlbernstein.com/
the-cia-and-the-media-rolling-stone-10-20-1977/

67 https://www.cesifo.org/DocDL/CESifo-Forum-2019-4-aslund-economic-sanctions-december.pdf/

68 https://carnegieendowment.org/2016/07/11/
role-of-sanctions-in-u.s.-russian-relations-pub-64056/

69 https://www.cnas.org/sanctions-by-the-numbers/

70 https://en.wikipedia.org/wiki/United_States_sanctions/

71 https://www.nationalww2museum.org/war/articles/
new-global-power-after-world-war-ii-1945/

72 https://www.state.gov/cuba-sanctions/

73 https://www.cfr.org/timeline/us-cuba-relations/

74 https://www.history.com/topics/cold-war/bay-of-pigs-invasion/

75 https://en.wikipedia.org/wiki/
United_States_grain_embargo_against_the_Soviet_Union/

76 https://www.foreignaffairs.com/articles/united-states/1980-09-01/
lessons-grain-embargo/

77 https://medium.com/insurge-intelligence/army-study-us-strategy-to-dethrone-putin-for-oil-pipelines-might-provoke-ww3-9b1d9dbe-6be9/

78 https://carnegieendowment.org/2016/07/11/
role-of-sanctions-in-u.s.-russian-relations-pub-64056/

79 https://foreignpolicy.com/2022/03/08/
swift-sanctions-ukraine-russia-nato-putin-war-global-finance/

80 https://som.yale.edu/story/2022/
over-1000-companies-have-curtailed-operations-russia-some-remain/

81 https://home.treasury.gov/news/press-releases/jy1494/

82 https://www.nbcnews.com/news/world/us-clear-warning-china-dont-come-russias-aid-will-beijing-heed-rcna20071/

83 https://www.nytimes.com/2023/02/22/us/politics/china-russia-sanctions.html/

84 https://www.theguardian.com/world/2023/apr/11/
us-and-philippines-launch-biggest-joint-drills-yet-in-south-china-sea/

85 Geopolitical Monitor Ukraine War: A reshuffling of the global Monetary Order? (May 17, 2022) https://www.geopoliticalmonitor.com/ukraine-war-a-reshuffling-of-the-global-monetary-order/

86 https://www.iwm.org.uk/history/the-naval-race-between-britain-and-germany-before-the-first-world-war/

87 https://theconversation.com/in-2014-the-decrepit-ukrainian-army-hit-the-refresh-button-eight-years-later-its-paying-off-177881/

88 U.S. Security Assistance to Ukraine Congressional Research Service (December 07, 2022)

89 https://www.statista.com/statistics/584286/
number-of-military-personnel-in-nato-countries/

90 https://www.globalfirepower.com/countries-comparison-detail.
php?country1=germany&country2=france/

91 https://www.statista.com/statistics/1296573/
russia-ukraine-military-comparison/

92 https://www.cato.org/commentary/washington-must-stop-challenging-other-major-powers-their-neighborhoods/

93 Id: See endnote #88.

94 U.S. Plans combined Arms Training for Ukraine Soldiers Dept of Defense News Dec 15, 2022.

95 https://www.everycrsreport.com/files/2020-10-23_R45307_db5e549ff7b735d26e5815d023c4fae694ac43de.pdf/

96 https://medium.com/insurge-intelligence/army-study-us-strategy-to-dethrone-putin-for-oil-pipelines-might-provoke-ww3-9b1d9dbe-6be9/

97 https://sgp.fas.org/crs/row/R45307.pdf/

98 https://stanjestvari.com/wp-content/uploads/2014/01/analiza-us-aid1.pdf/

99 https://www.firstpost.com/opinion/how-george-soros-attempts-to-further-his-anarchist-ideas-spawned-political-instability-in-post-soviet-states-12462062.html/

100 https://www.euronews.com/2018/08/07/europe-s-forgotten-war-the-georgia-russia-conflict-explained-a-decade-on/

101 Ibid: See endnote #99.

102 https://www.geopolicalmonitor.com/us-incites-georgia-august-11-2008-1015/

103 https://www.gsb.stanford.edu/insights/what-elite-donors-want/

104 https://www.eisenhowerlibrary.gov/research/online-documents/farewell-address/

105 President Dwight D. Eisenhower's Farewell Address/U.S. NATIONAL ARCHIVES January 17, 1961

106 www.washingtonexaminer.com/news/white-house/spy-budgets-soared-in-trumps-first-year/

107 www.washingtonpost.com/wp-srv/special/national/black-budget/

108 https://thediplomat.com/2013/08/us-intelligence-community-the-worlds-4th-largest-military/

109 https://thediplomat.com/2013/08/
us-intelligence-community-the-worlds-4th-largest-military/

110 https://www.macrotrends.net/countries/USA/united-states/
military-spending-defense-budget/

111 https://www.visualcapitalist.com/
mapped-largest-military-budgets-2022/

112 https://www.macrotrends.net/countries/RUS/russia/
military-spending-defense-budget/

113 America's Ukraine Hypocrisy CATO Commentary by Ted Galen
Carpenter (August 6, 2017)

114 https://militarytruth.org/wp-content/uploads/2018/03/American-
Interference-in-Foreign-Affairs.pdf/

115 Ibid: See endnote #112.

116 https://reason.com/2022/07/15/boltons-coup-boast-under-
mines-election-interference-complaints/?comments=true#comments/

117 https://journals.sagepub.com/doi/
pdf/10.1177/0738894216661190/

118 Fighting a culture of corruption in Ukraine, Carnegie Europe by
Thomas de Waal (April 18, 2016)

119 The Obama regime's plan to seize the Russian Naval Base in
Crimea By Eric Zuesse, The Liberty Beacon (January 26, 2023)

120 https://apps.dtic.mil/sti/tr/pdf/ADA494885.pdf/

121 https://www.reuters.com/article/us-ukraine-russia-deal-special-
report/special-report-why-ukraine-spurned-the-eu-and-embraced-
russia-idUSBRE9BI0DZ20131219/

122 https://www.cato.org/commentary/americas-ukraine-hypocrisy#/

123 A US backed far Right led Revolution in Ukraine helped bring
us to the brink of war by Branko Marcetic: Jacobin US meddling in

the political affairs of other nations is well documented and common modus operandi by U.S. American Foreign Policy.

124 https://world.time.com/2014/02/22/ ukraines-president-flees-protestors-capture-kiev/

125 Ukraine will remain a neutral state Speech by Viktor Yanukovych Kiev Post (January 07, 2010)

126 https://www.cato.org/commentary/americas-ukraine-hypocrisy#/

127 https://www.c-span.org/video/?316878-1/ senator-john-mccain-ukraine/

128 https://jacobin.com/2022/02/ maidan-protests-neo-nazis-russia-nato-crimea/

129 https://truthout.org/articles/the-ukraine-mess-that-nuland-made/

130 https://www.washingtonexamin- er.com/policy/defense-national-security/ us-aid-to-ukraine-tops-112-billion-in-year-one/

131 Washington is prolonging Ukraine's suffering by Colonel Douglas Macgrgor: Foreign Affairs (December 20, 2022)

132 Statisca (2023)

133 https://www.crfb.org/blogs/ congress-approved-113-billion-aid-ukraine-2022/

134 https://doi.org/10.1177%2F0022002718770507; https://carnegieendowment.org/2018/03/12/ is-u.s.-hypocritical-to-criticize-russian-election-meddling-pub-75780/

135 https://www.justsecurity.org/81313/ still-at-war-the-united-states-in-syria/

136 Timeline: Euromaidan, the original Ukraine Crisis by Kit Knightly, Offguardian (February 24, 2022)

137 Ukrainian military total expenditure in 2021 before the conflict was approx. $6 Billion dollars with total GDP approx. $200 Billion dollars. See Statistica 2023

138 Intel Sharing between U.S. and Ukraine "Revolutionary" says DIA Director BY John Grady USNI News (March 18, 2022)

139 https://www.nbcnews.com/politics/national-security/us-intel-helped-ukraine-sink-russian-flagship-moskva-officials-say-rc-na27559/

140 Susan Rice says Russia should not involve troops in Ukraine: The Washington Post By Josh Hicks (February 23, 2022)

141 Ukraine signed the European Ukraine Association Agreement on June 27, 2014. This formal agreement provided a comprehensive free trade area between Ukraine and EU members. Russia invaded Ukraine on February 24, 2022, fully eight years later. Obviously, Ukraine's trade with the West was NOT the primary cause and did not trigger the current military confrontation by Russia.

142 https://truthout.org/articles/us-provides-military-assistance-to-73-percent-of-world-s-dictatorships/

143 https://www.theguardian.com/news/2015/feb/04/welcome-to-the-most-corrupt-nation-in-europe-ukraine/

144 https://news.un.org/en/story/2021/12/1107972/

145 https://thehill.com/policy/international/europe/598952-zelensky-says-ukrainian-political-parties-linked-to-russia-banned/

146 https://www.livemint.com/news/world/no-presidential-election-in-ukraine-till-war-ends-zelensky-11687799430295.html/

147 https://www.npr.org/2019/12/18/788874844/how-u-s-military-aid-has-helped-ukraine-since-2014/

148 Washington helped Trigger the Ukraine War by Ted Galen Carpenter: The Cato Institute (March 25, 2022)

149 https://theconversation.com/crimea-ukraine-uses-new-tactics-to-attempt-to-take-back-strategic-territory-from-russia-188951/

150 https://mronline.org/2021/04/08/why-ukraines-borders-are-back-at-the-center-of-geopolitics/

151 How a Ukrainian Dam played a key role in tensions with Russia: The Hill by Sharon Udasin (March 12, 2022)

152 https://www.reuters.com/article/us-ukraine-parliament-language/ukraine-passes-language-law-irritating-president-elect-and-russia-idUSKCN1S111N/

153 https://www.forbes.com/sites/davidaxe/2023/06/05/ukraine-aims-to-cut-off-russian-troops-in-crimea-kyivs-new-snow-tractors-could-make-it-possible/?sh=1d9e68ce10f3/

154 https://www.history.co.uk/articles/putin-s-gamble-russia-s-2014-invasion-of-crimea/

155 https://www.rferl.org/a/ukraine-crimea-ethnic-divisions/25268159.html/

156 https://en.wikipedia.org/wiki/Annexation_of_the_Crimean_Khanate_by_the_Russian_Empire/

157 https://www.history.com/news/ukraine-timeline-invasions/

158 https://www.crisisgroup.org/content/conflict-ukraines-donbas-visual-explainer/

159 https://www.aljazeera.com/news/2014/5/12/ukraine-separatists-declare-independence/

160 Ukraine Conflict: Bombing, shelling in populated areas cause incredible suffering for civilians:

161 IBID see mapping Azoz Movement Stanford Review above Pages 5-6 (endnote #5).

162 Setting the record straight-stuff you should know about Ukraine by Mike Whitney (February 11, 2023)

163 https://www.reuters.com/article/us-ukraine-parliament-language/ukraine-passes-language-law-irritating-president-elect-and-russia-idUSKCN1S111N/

164 https://www.brookings.edu/articles/1979-iran-and-america/

165 Ukraine appeals to the world for help keeping the lights on http://www.nbcnews.com/

166 https://www.ndtv.com/world-news/comedian-volodymyr-zelensky-with-no-political-record-leads-ukraines-presidential-election-2026438/

167 https://www.rferl.org/a/zelenskiys-first-year-he-promised-sweeping-changes-how-s-he-doing-/30576329.html/

168 Id: See endnote #164.

169 Independent Ukraine's free speech is under threat: The Atlantic (December 08, 2021) Media law signed by Zelensky could restrict press freedom in Ukraine: The New York Times By Anushka Patil (December 30, 2022)

170 "Ukrainian peace negotiator is shot dead" at Daily Mail.com (March 6, 2022). The murder was carried out by Ukraine's security service. Of course, the official Ukrainian position is that he was a Russian Spy and resisted arrest.

171 CNE.News, Zelensky takes further steps against Ukrainian Orthodox Church: Christian Network Europe (December 14, 2022)

172 https://moderndiplomacy.eu/2023/01/29/zelensky-regime-war-against-the-ukrainian-orthodox-church/

173 Ukraine's corruption is well documented. See Fighting a culture of corruption in Ukraine Carnegie Europe by Thomas de Waal (April 18, 2016)

174 https://www.theguardian.com/world/2022/jun/02/ukraine-weapons-end-up-criminal-hands-says-interpol-chief-jurgen-stock/

175 https://www.occrp.org/en/the-pandora-papers/pandora-papers-reveal-offshore-holdings-of-ukrainian-president-and-his-inner-circ/

176 https://www.eurasiantimes.com/ukraine-war-zelensky-embezzled-400-million-allocated-by-the-us-for-purchasing-fuel-seymour-hersh/

177 https://medium.com/@deborahlarmstrong/zelenskys-5-million-villa-in-egypt-fe3f80f76940/

178 https://militarywatchmagazine.com/article/ukraine-conscripts-wsj-meatgrinders/

179 https://www.defense.gov/News/News-Stories/Article/Article/3370802/milley-says-ukraine-has-leadership-morale-to-beat-russia/#:~:text=Milley%20said%20the%20Ukrainian%20forces,and%20shelling%20of%20urban%20areas/

180 https://www.whitehouse.gov/briefing-room/speeches-remarks/2023/02/20/remarks-by-president-biden-and-president-zelenskyy-of-ukraine-in-joint-statement/

181 https://www.businessinsider.com/top-us-general-says-russia-has-lost-the-ukraine-war-2023-2/

182 https://www.ny1.com/nyc/all-boroughs/news/2023/07/13/biden-helsinki-finland-nato/

183 https://www.economist.com/the-economist-explains/2022/12/20/is-russia-running-out-of-ammunition/

184 Unless of course, America and the West supplies military aircraft and introduces troops into Ukraine. However, to do so would lengthen the war and greatly increases the odds that the world would become embroiled in WWIII.

185 https://www.npr.org/2023/07/28/1190544651/ukraine-rebuild-navy-destroyed-by-russia

186 Id: https://www.csis.org/blogs/development-dispatch/road-recovery-ukraines-economic-challenges-and-opportunities.

187 Russia-Ukraine Casualties, The Times Examiner (January 23, 2023)

188 http://infobrics.org/post/39192

189 https://www.archives.gov/research/military/vietnam-war/casualty-statistics/

190 https://english.elpais.com/international/2023-03-01/ukraine-outgunned-10-to-1-in-massive-artillery-battle-with-russia.html/

191 Current migration flows from Ukraine: Center for research and Analysis of Migration (January 17, 2023)

192 http://www.nbcnews.com Ukraine appeals to the world for help keeping the lights on (January 20, 2023)

193 https://www.pbs.org/newshour/world/russia-almost-fully-in-control-of-donbas-province-now-holds-20-percent-of-ukraine/

194 A struggle to survive Ukraine's economy in wartime OSW Commentary By Stawomir Matuszak (October 18, 2022)

195 The Cost of War: Carnegie Endowment for international Peace By Alexandra Prokopenko (December 19, 2022)

196 Officially, Russia in late 2022 is reporting only 10,000 casualties while western sources report higher than 100,000. See The Moscow Times by Yanina Sorokina (December16, 2022) in contrast with official Pentagon estimates of 80,000 military casualties: See http://military.com daily news 2022/08/08.

197 https://theconversation.com/putins-state-of-the-nation-why-russia-hasnt-officially-declared-war-and-what-difference-it-would-make-200208/

198 https://en.as.com/en/2022/02/24/latest_news/1645729870_894320.html/

199 https://www.reuters.com/world/europe/russias-partial-mobilisation-will-see-300000-drafted-defence-minister-2022-09-21/

200 It is sheer spin and propaganda that Russia seeks to conquer the entire territory of Ukraine and resurrect the old Soviet empire. This is obvious from Russia's annual expenditures on its military. In 2019 total Russian military expenditures were approximately 48 Billion dollars. In stark contrast, NATO total expenditures totaled almost 1 trillion dollars—fully 1500% more than Russia. See http://worldpopulationreview.com defense-spending-by-country.

201 Of course, the West prefers a stalemate to suffering flat out defeat. However, this is a land war and Russian forces hold significant advantages and ability to place more boots on the ground than Ukraine as well as the advantage of fighting from the interior lines. Without NATO introducing boots on the ground as well, a Russian victory is a certainty. In the event the war expands, Russian air defenses and air force can largely neutralize NATO's airpower.

202 Wilson Center, Insight & Analysis Countries that have sanctioned Russia by Ambassador Mark Green (May 10, 202)

203 Hungary, Serbia agree to build pipeline to ship Russian oil to Servia: Reuters (October 10, 2022)

204 https://www.wsj.com/articles/switzerland-becomes-stumbling-block-for-western-military-aid-to-ukraine-6003880c

205 https://thegrayzone.com/2023/02/27/europeans-protest-natos-proxy-war/

206 https://www.euronews.com/my-europe/2022/02/26/ukraine-war-thousands-across-europe-protest-over-russia-s-invasion/. This typical report in European press is absent in America.

207 https://foreignpolicy.com/2022/02/18/us-russia-china-war-nato-quadrilateral-security-dialogue/

208 https://www.bloomberg.com/news/articles/2023-07-20/brics-expansion-plan-draws-interest-from-more-than-40-nations#xj4y7vzkg

209 https://apnews.com/article/brics-russia-china-summit-b5900168d165cc78b36d5d5c068b7a50/

210 Russia blocked Russia-Ukraine Peace Process says former Israeli PM by Dave DeCamp at Antiwar.com Congressional Progressive caucus letter to President Biden dated October 24, 2022, requesting immediate negotiations to end the Ukrainian conflict signed by thirty members in Congress.

211 https://www.csis.org/analysis/united-states-aid-ukraine-investment-whose-benefits-greatly-exceed-its-cost/

212https://www.euronews.com/green/2023/02/24/europes-energy-war-in-data-how-have-eu-imports-changed-since-russias-invasion-of-ukraine/

213 Senator Graham calls for somebody in Russia to take Putin Out: (March 04, 2022)

214 Id: See endnote #192.

215 Id: See endnote #5.

216 Historically, Germany and Russia have been major trading partners. This of course is seen by some, including American elites, as a threat to their interests in the region.

217 https://www.cfr.org/backgrounder/ukraine-conflict-crossroads-europe-and-russia/

218 https://groovyhistory.com/follow-the-money-quote-all-the-presidents-men/2

219 U.S. top send another $3 Billion Dollars in military aid including Bradley vehicles; Business World (January 26, 2023)

220 https://apnews.com/article/biden-ukraine-f16-decision-russia-64538af7c10489d7c2243dadbad31008/

221 https://www.wilsoncenter.org/blog-post/putins-miscalculations/

222 https://responsiblestatecraft.org/2022/09/02/diplomacy-watch-why-did-the-west-stop-a-peace-deal-in-ukraine/

223 Diplomacy, Restraint, and Luck: How Kennedy and Khrushchev avoided Nuclear Disaster By Elissa Karim http://www.globalzero.org/ (October 27, 2016

224 https://www.revolutionarydemocracy.org/rdv17n1/usdollar.htm/

225 https://www.aljazeera.com/news/2021/9/10/ infographic-us-military-presence-around-the-world-interactive/

About the Author

Terry Hyten was born and raised in Peoria, Illinois. He earned a Bachelor of Science Degree from Bradley University in Peoria, Illinois in1978. He then earned a Juris Doctorate Degree from The John Marshall Law School in 1982 and is licensed to practice law in both Illinois and Missouri in state and federal court. He has argued in both Appellate and in the Illinois Supreme Court. He was also elected to and served as Trustee for the Village of Prairie Grove from 2001 through 2005, fulfilling a call to civic responsibility. It is his latest call to civic duty to which he places pen to paper and writes this book.